The New School @ South Shore
8825 Rainier Ave. South
Seattle, WA 98118

The Way People Live

Life Among the Inca

THE WAY PEOPLE LIVE

Life Among the
Inca

Titles in The Way People Live series include:

Cowboys in the Old West
Games of Ancient Rome
Life Aboard the Space Shuttle
Life Aboard the Space Station
Life Among the Aztec
Life Among the Great Plains Indians
Life Among the Ibo Women of Nigeria
Life Among the Indian Fighters
Life Among the Pirates
Life Among the Puritans
Life Among the Samurai
Life Among the Vikings
Life During the American Revolution
Life During the Black Death
Life During the Crusades
Life During the French Revolution
Life During the Gold Rush
Life During the Great Depression
Life During the Middle Ages
Life During the Renaissance
Life During the Roaring Twenties
Life During the Russian Revolution
Life During the Spanish Inquisition
Life in a Japanese American Internment Camp
Life in a Medieval Castle
Life in a Medieval Monastery
Life in a Medieval Village
Life in America During the 1960s
Life in an Amish Community
Life in a Nazi Concentration Camp
Life in Ancient Athens
Life in Ancient China
Life in Ancient Egypt
Life in Ancient Greece
Life in Ancient Rome
Life in a Wild West Show
Life in Berlin
Life in Castro's Cuba
Life in Charles Dickens's England
Life in Communist Russia
Life in Genghis Khan's Mongolia
Life in Hong Kong
Life in Moscow
Life in the Amazon Rain Forest
Life in the American Colonies
Life in the Australian Outback
Life in the Elizabethan Theater
Life in the Hitler Youth
Life in the Negro Baseball League
Life in the North During the Civil War
Life in the South During the Civil War
Life in the Warsaw Ghetto
Life in Tokyo
Life in War-Torn Bosnia
Life of a Medieval Knight
Life of a Nazi Soldier
Life of a Roman Gladiator
Life of a Roman Slave
Life of a Roman Soldier
Life of a Slave on a Southern Plantation
Life on Alcatraz
Life on a Medieval Pilgrimage
Life on an African Slave Ship
Life on an Everest Expedition
Life on a New World Voyage
Life in an Indian Reservation
Life on Ellis Island
Life on the American Frontier
Life on the Oregon Trail
Life on the Pony Express
Life on the Underground Railroad
Life Under the Jim Crow Laws
Lifr Under the Taliban

THE WAY PEOPLE LIVE

Life Among the
Inca

by James A. Corrick

LUCENT BOOKS®

THOMSON
✦
GALE

San Diego • Detroit • New York • San Francisco • Cleveland • New Haven, Conn. • Waterville, Maine • London • Munich

THOMSON
★
GALE

© 2004 by Lucent Books ®. Lucent Books ® is an imprint of Thomson Gale, a part of the Thomson Corporation.

Thomson is a trademark and Gale [and Lucent Books] are registered trademarks used herein under license.

For more information, contact
Lucent Books
27500 Drake Rd.
Farmington Hills, MI 48331-3535
Or you can visit our Internet site at http://www.gale.com

ALL RIGHTS RESERVED.
No part of this work covered by the copyright hereon may be reproduced or used in any form or by any means—graphic, electronic, or mechanical, including photocopying, recording, taping, Web distribution, or information storage retrieval systems—without the written permission of the publisher.

LIBRARY OF CONGRESS CATALOGING-IN-PUBLICATION DATA

Corrick, James A.
  Life among the Inca / by James A. Corrick.
    p. cm. — (The way people live)
  Contents: An ordered world—Bureaucrats and taxpayers—Private life—Priests and worshippers—Working life—Army life—The builders.
  Includes bibliographical references and index.
  ISBN 1-59018-161-1 (lib. bdg. : alk. paper)
  1. Incas—History. 2. Incas—Social life and customs. I. Title. II. Series.
  F3429.C68 2004
  985'.019—dc22
                                                      2004010207

Printed in the United States of America

Contents

FOREWORD
    Discovering the Humanity in Us All   8

INTRODUCTION
    A High-Altitude Civilization   10

CHAPTER ONE
    An Ordered World   14

CHAPTER TWO
    Bureaucrats and Taxpayers   22

CHAPTER THREE
    Private Life   34

CHAPTER FOUR
    Priests and Worshippers   46

CHAPTER FIVE
    Working Life   60

CHAPTER SIX
    Army Life   70

CHAPTER SEVEN
    The Builders   80

EPILOGUE
    The End of Empire   92

    Notes   95
    For Further Reading   98
    Works Consulted   100
    Index   103
    Picture Credits   111
    About the Author   112

Foreword

Discovering the Humanity in Us All

Books in The Way People Live series focus on groups of people in a wide variety of circumstances, settings, and time periods. Some books focus on different cultural groups, others on people in a particular historical time period, while others cover people involved in a specific event. Each book emphasizes the daily routines, personal and historical struggles, and achievements of people from all walks of life.

To really understand any culture, it is necessary to strip the mind of the common notions we hold about groups of people. These stereotypes are the archenemies of learning. It does not even matter whether the stereotypes are positive or negative; they are confining and tight. Removing them is a challenge that is not easily met, as anyone who has ever tried it will admit. Ideas that do not fit into the templates we create are unwelcome visitors—ones we would prefer remain quietly in a corner or forgotten room.

The cowboy of the Old West is a good example of such confining roles. The cowboy was courageous, yet soft-spoken. His time (it is always a he, in our template) was spent alternatively saving a rancher's daughter from certain death on a runaway stagecoach, or shooting it out with rustlers. At times, of course, he was likely to get a little crazy in town after a trail drive, but for the most part, he was the epitome of inner strength. It is disconcerting to find out that the cowboy is human, even a bit childish. Can it really be true that cowboys would line up to help the cook on the trail drive grind coffee, just hoping he would give them a little stick of peppermint candy that came with the coffee shipment? The idea of tough cowboys vying with one another to help "Coosie" (as they called their cooks) for a bit of candy seems silly and out of place.

So is the vision of Eskimos playing video games and watching MTV, living in prefab housing in the Arctic. It just does not fit with what "Eskimo" means. We are far more comfortable with snow igloos and whale blubber, harpoons and kayaks.

Although the cultures dealt with in Lucent's The Way People Live series are often historically and socially well known, the emphasis is on the personal aspects of life. Groups of people, while unquestionably affected by their politics and their governmental structures, are more than those institutions. How do people in a particular time and place educate their children? What do they eat? And how do they build their houses? What kinds of work do they do? What kinds of games do they enjoy? The answers to these questions bring these cultures to life. People's lives are revealed in the particulars and only by knowing the particulars can we understand these cultures' will to survive and their moments of weakness and greatness.

This is not to say that understanding politics does not help to understand a culture. There is no question that the Warsaw ghetto, for example, was a culture that was brought about by the politics and social ideas of Adolf

Hitler and the Third Reich. But the Jews who were crowded together in the ghetto cannot be understood by the Reich's politics. Their life was a day-to-day battle for existence, and the creativity and methods they used to prolong their lives is a vital story of human perseverance that would be denied by focusing only on the institutions of Hitler's Germany. Knowing that children as young as five or six outwitted Nazi guards on a daily basis, that Jewish policemen helped the Germans control the ghetto, that children attended secret schools in the ghetto and even earned diplomas—these are the things that reveal the fabric of life, that can inspire, intrigue, and amaze.

Books in The Way People Live series allow both the casual reader and the student to see humans as victims, heroes, and onlookers. And although humans act in ways that can fill us with feelings of sorrow and revulsion, it is important to remember that "hero," "predator," and "victim" are dangerous terms. Heaping undue pity or praise on people reduces them to objects, and strips them of their humanity.

Seeing the Jews of Warsaw only as victims is to deny their humanity. Seeing them only as they appear in surviving photos, staring at the camera with infinite sadness, is limiting, both to them and to those who want to understand them. To an object of pity, the only appropriate response becomes "Those poor creatures!" and that reduces both the quality of their struggle and the depth of their despair. No one is served by such two-dimensional views of people and their cultures.

With this in mind, The Way People Live series strives to flesh out the traditional, two-dimensional views of people in various cultures and historical circumstances. Using a wide variety of primary quotations—the words not only of the politicians and government leaders, but of the real people whose lives are being examined—each book in the series attempts to show an honest and complete picture of a culture removed from our own by time or space.

By examining cultures in this way, the reader will notice not only the glaring differences from his or her own culture, but also will be struck by the similarities. For indeed, people share common needs—warmth, good company, stability, and affirmation from others. Ultimately, seeing how people really live, or have lived, can only enrich our understanding of ourselves.

Introduction: A High-Altitude Civilization

South America was the home of one of the great civilizations of the Western Hemisphere: the Inca Empire. At its height at the beginning of the sixteenth century, the empire was a rich, mighty domain that stretched some two thousand miles from what is now southern Colombia to central Chile. Its western border was the Pacific Ocean; much of its eastern boundary was the Amazon rain forest. In between, the empire included Pacific coastal lands and the slopes and highlands of the Andes mountains.

The Inca Empire was so large that out of its vast territory would come the modern nations of Bolivia, Peru, and Ecuador, as well as parts of Colombia, Chile, and Argentina. Commenting on the incredible size of the Incan state, archaeologist Michael E. Moseley writes,

> On the eve of [European explorer Christopher] Columbus' ... landfall [in the Americas in 1493] it [the Inca Empire] probably surpassed ... China and the Ottoman Empire as the largest nation on earth.... It was the biggest native state to arise in the western hemisphere, and also the largest empire of antiquity ever to develop south of the equator.... No contemporary [present-day] ... Andean State compares in magnitude or prosperity.[1]

The Incan Homeland

The Inca Empire arose in the Andes. Stretching the full length of South America, the Andes are a towering, rugged mountain range, with many peaks topping twenty-one thousand feet. Only the tallest mountains of the Himalayas in Asia are higher.

The Andes pose many challenges to humans trying to live at high altitudes. Thin air makes physical activity difficult, and steep slopes guarantee the danger of bad falls and landslides. The range is also a land of ice and fire. Glaciers flow slowly down the sides of many Andean peaks, extending tongues of ice into mountain lakes and rivers. Many active volcanoes are found in the Andes as well, and the same geologic forces that give rise to the volcanoes also produce devastating earthquakes.

Yet there is habitable, fertile ground among these mountains. Many plateaus nestled among the Andes' peaks contain valleys, lakes, marshes, and flat open plains. Having trekked through the region, sixteenth-century Spanish soldier Pedro de Cieza de León wrote,

> In the openings and plains of the highlands of the Andes ... there are large settlements where there were and are many people, because through these valleys run rivers of excellent water.... If it were not for them, it would be impossible for people to live there.... [Otherwise,] they would all perish of hunger and cold.[2]

In one of these valleys, located in modern-day Peru, the earliest Incan tribes settled and founded the village of Cuzco. Then, around 1400 the Incas began conquering their neighbors in the first step toward building an empire.

The Land of the Four Quarters

The rise of the Inca Empire was explosive. In a little over a century, the Incas conquered the Andean region that makes up much of western South America. Then, as suddenly as their empire building began, it ended when the Incas fell victim to other conquerors—the Spanish conquistadors—in 1532.

During the century of expansion, four Incan rulers led the Incas to victory after victory: Viracocha Inca (ca. 1400–1438), Pachacuti Inca Yupanqui (1438–1471), Topa Inca Yupanqui (1471–1493), and Huayna Capac (1493–1527). These leaders were not only warriors, they were also builders. They turned Cuzco from a village of huts and small houses into a great city filled with monumental buildings that awed not only their subjects but also their Spanish conquerors. In addition to Cuzco, the Incan rulers built at least a dozen other cities, and conquered many urban centers (the exact number of Incan cities is unknown).

The Incas called their empire Tahuantinsuyu (sometimes spelled Tawantinsuyu), or the Land of the Four Quarters, because it was

The Incas first settled in the highlands of the Andes mountains, in the shadow of snow-covered peaks that rise more than twenty thousand feet.

A High-Altitude Civilization

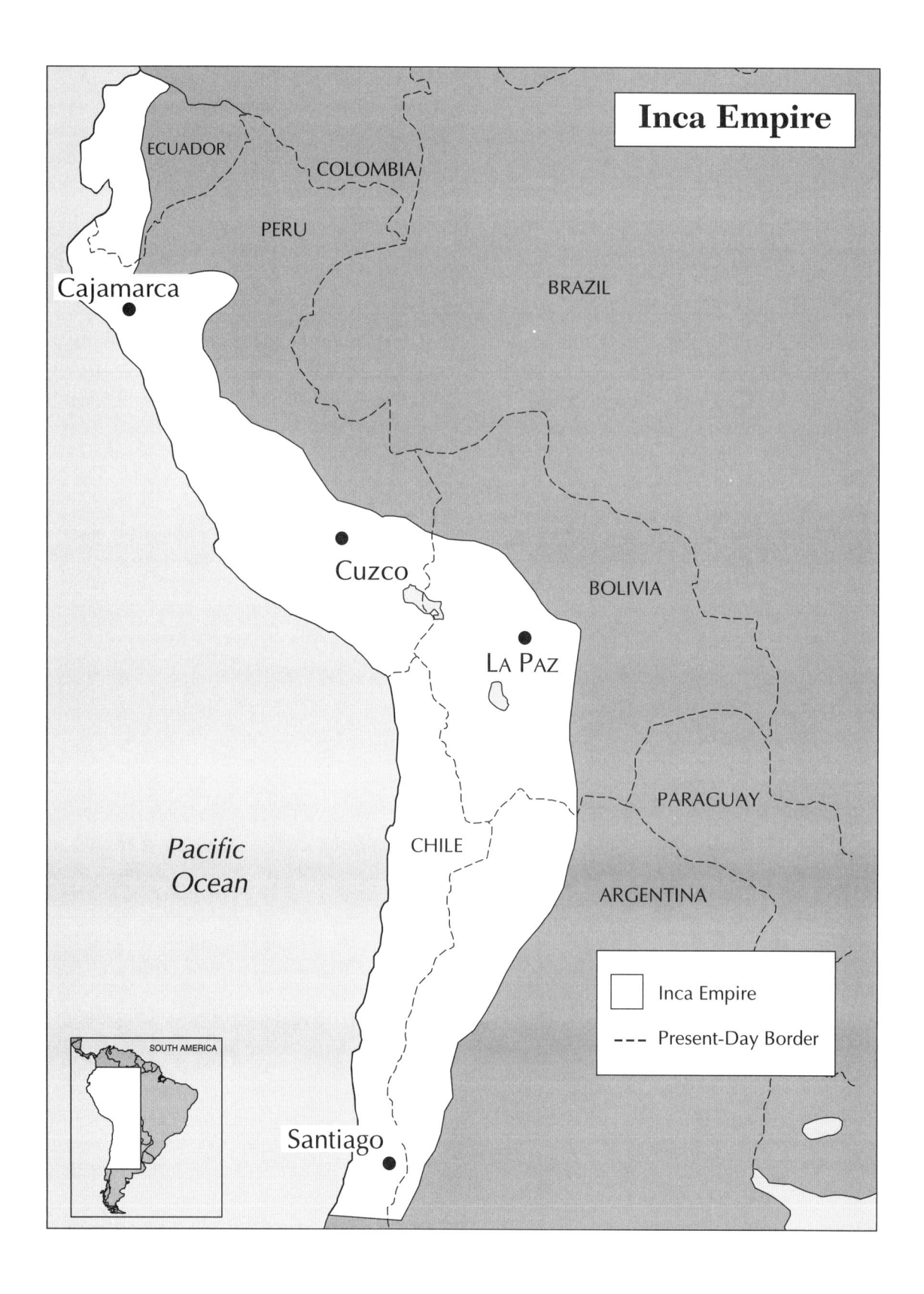

Inca Empire

- Cajamarca
- Cuzco
- La Paz
- Santiago

ECUADOR
COLOMBIA
PERU
BRAZIL
BOLIVIA
PARAGUAY
CHILE
ARGENTINA

Pacific Ocean

SOUTH AMERICA

Legend:
- ☐ Inca Empire
- --- Present-Day Border

divided into four main sections. According to scholar Brian M. Fagan, "Four highways from Cuzco's central plaza divided the kingdom into four *suyu* [quarters], which were themselves linked to the four quarters of the Incan heaven."[3] Reflecting its central position in the Incan realm, Cuzco in Quechua, the Incan language, means "navel."

An Orderly and Efficient Society

Some 10 million people lived within the Inca Empire. They were a mix of more than one hundred ethnic groups who spoke twenty different languages. The true Incas, however, numbered perhaps as few as forty thousand. They were the aristocrats of the empire, and their leader was the emperor, known as the Inca.

From Cuzco, Incan rulers kept tight control over the affairs and lives of their millions of subjects. They provided an efficient system of government. Incan officials dispensed justice and furnished military protection from hostile neighbors as well.

The Incan government was dedicated to providing for its subjects. Thus, no one in the empire wanted; no one had to beg for necessities. Each person, no matter how lowly, had enough food, decent clothing, and proper housing. The empire could easily afford this generosity. Efficient management of its economy had made it wealthy. Indeed, its aristocratic homes were full of luxuries.

To maintain the empire's wealth, Incas at all levels of society worked. The aristocrats were government officials and top army officers. The rest of the people worked the farms and mines and constructed the public buildings and roads. Incan officials scheduled all this necessary community work and ensured that it was carried out.

The Incas, however, were more than savvy administrators and hard workers. They were also skilled engineers and talented artisans. They built their cities of stone and laid down paved roads that gave them swift access to all parts of the realm. And they produced superior gold and silver artifacts, as well as fine textiles.

The Sources

Despite their many achievements, the Incas produced no written records of their history or of their way of life, for they did not have a system of writing. However, in the years after the Incas' fall, many Spanish writers, fascinated by the people they had subdued, wrote chronicles that detail those lives. These accounts are based on the authors' firsthand experiences in the former empire and on interviews with the Incan people. Some of the writers, such as Garcilaso de la Vega, were part Inca.

In addition to these writings, archaeologists have discovered further information about the way the Incas lived. The chronicles and the archaeological finds give a glimpse into the world of the Incas. The resulting picture reveals a rich, vibrant, and fascinating society that was healthy and growing when the Spanish arrived in 1532. And, although the Inca Empire ended with the Spanish Conquest, much of Incan society—language, social organization, and farming, among other things—survived to be passed down to the present-day descendants of the Incas.

CHAPTER 1

An Ordered World

Incan society was an ordered one, made of social classes and family groupings. It was organized as a pyramid, with the emperor at its apex and the common people at the bottom. In between was the aristocracy. Everyone had a place, and everyone knew what that place was. Indeed, there was little social mobility. One was born into a class and died in that class.

The Unique Inca

The emperor was officially known as the Sapa Inca, or the Unique Inca. Because he represented his people and his empire, he was sometimes simply referred to as the Inca. His authority rested first on his claim of being a direct descendant of the legendary Inca founder, Manco Capac, and second, on his claim of being related to the Sun, one of the major deities of the Incan state religion. Thus, the Sapa Inca was divine and ruled by divine right. He was an absolute monarch whose word was law. No one could contradict him; no one could countermand him.

The emperor's life was one of absolute privilege. Whatever he wanted, he received. For example, the Spanish missionary Martin de Murúa wrote in 1590,

> When the Inca wished to eat fresh fish from the sea, and as it was seventy or eighty leagues [210 or 240 miles] from the coast to Cuzco . . . , they were brought [by runners] alive and twitching, which seems incredible over such a long distance over such rough and craggy roads, but they [runners] ran on foot, not on horseback, because they never had horses until the Spanish came to this country [Peru].[4]

Imperial Presence

The emperor cut an imposing figure that was meant to awe his subjects with his might and power. To emphasize his rank, he dressed in the finest wool clothing available. A sleeveless, knee-length tunic covered his upper body, and striped trousers fit his legs. A cloak, often white in color and generally decorated with geometric designs, hung down his back, and he wore white wool sandals on his feet.

The Inca never wore the same garments twice and often changed his clothes several times a day. While visiting the emperor Atahuallpa in 1533, the Spanish conquistador Francisco Pizarro saw a piece of food fall on the Inca's clothes. Atahuallpa "rose and went into his chamber to change," wrote Pizarro. The emperor returned "wearing a dark brown tunic and cloak. . . . The cloak . . . was softer than silk. He explained that it was made from the skins of bats."[5]

To further indicate his rank, the emperor wore a braided, multicolored headband with red fringe. From the fringe dangled gold tubes and red tassels. Also symbolizing the Inca's rank were disks of gold inserted in holes in each earlobe.

Life Among the Inca

Imperial Audience

During important ceremonies, the Inca held a long staff made of gold, and a golden disk that represented the sun hung from his neck. He sat on a throne made of solid gold or, when traveling, on a wooden chair covered with carvings and padded with decorated cloth.

Even the highest ranking members of society had to humble themselves before the emperor. Scholar Ann Kendall notes that "a person desiring to come into the Sapa Inca's presence, whatever his rank, took off his . . . sandals and put a token burden on his back as a sign of respect."[6] The audience seeker spoke with lowered eyes. The emperor was often seated behind a screen, and if he spoke, his speech was brief. Sometimes he relayed his messages through another person. All of these actions emphasized the Inca's godlike remoteness from all other people.

By Blood and by Privilege

Directly below the emperor on the social pyramid were the rest of the Incan tribe. Only

As a descendant of the sun god, the Incan emperor ruled as an absolute monarch by divine right. Pictured is Atahuallpa, the last Incan emperor.

members of groups living in and around the valley that contained the Incan capital of Cuzco were considered Incas. They all spoke a common language, Quechua. All of the remaining peoples of the empire were Incan subjects. The Spanish failed to understand this difference and called any Andean native Incan or Peruvian.

Among the native Incas, there were two classes: Incas-by-blood and Incas-by-privilege. Incas-by-blood were either relatives of the emperor or members of the valley population who were not related to the imperial family. Incas-by-privilege belonged to groups living near the Cuzco Valley.

All Incas, whether by blood or privilege, were part of the imperial aristocracy, although the former were of higher rank. The Incas' position, historian Nigel Davies writes, "was unassailable and immutable [unchanging]. . . . [They] were exempt from taxes. . . . They were supported by the king [Sapa Inca] through his revenues."[7] This elite never performed manual labor; the necessary work to keep Cuzco a functioning city was done by non-Incas who were imported for just this purpose.

Incas had many special privileges. They had the right to wear a headband, although one that lacked the red fringe of the Sapa Inca's headband. Also, the aristocracy wore disks in their ears, though somewhat smaller than those of the emperor. The seventeenth-century Spanish chronicler Fernando Montesinos explained that the emperor "honoured the men . . . by permitting them to bore their ears . . . , which were brought gradually to half the size of those of [the Inca]; and this was the sign of nobility."[8]

Moreover, the aristocracy was allowed to own luxury goods. They wore fine clothing, ate off gold and silver plates, soled their sandals in silver, and carpeted their homes with wool tapestries. So they might have the time to enjoy

The First Inca

Manco Capac was the legendary first ruler of the Incas, and a number of different versions of his story exist. The following one is found in *Black Rainbow*, edited by John Bierhorst.

"In ages long past . . . the people lived like beasts. . . . Our Father the Sun took pity on them and sent down from the sky his own son and daughter . . . to show them how to build villages, grow crops, and tend livestock.

Our Father the Sun sent his two children down to Lake Titicaca and ordered them to proceed from there. . . . Wherever they stopped . . . they were to push in the ground a rod of gold. . . . Wherever the rod could be made to disappear in the earth with a single thrust [there] . . . they would found their city. . . .

Our lord, the Inca [Manco Capac], . . . proceeded with his sister and wife . . . to the Valley of Cuzco. . . . The first stop they made in this valley was at the hill called Rainbow, on the south side of the present city. There they tried the earth with the rod of gold, and with a single stroke they drove it in and it was not seen again. . . .

Our first rulers went out from the hill. . . . As they proceeded through the wilderness they told all the men and women they met how their Father the Sun had sent them from the sky to be rulers. . . . They [the people] believed what they were told and adored the Inca. . . . They . . . followed where our rulers led them. . . .

These then were the first beginnings of the city you see today. . . . Our first Inca was called Manco Capac."

their luxury, they were permitted servants to tend to their houses and their land.

The Commoners

At the bottom of Incan society were the common people, who made up the bulk of the imperial population. These people were all members of cultures who had been conquered by the Incas. They served as the empire's farmers, laborers, servants, ordinary soldiers, and even skilled artisans.

Commoners led a very restricted life. They were forbidden to possess anything more than was absolutely necessary to meet their basic needs: plain clothing, cooking gear, and tools. All other items were considered luxury goods that only the royal family and the Incan aristocracy could possess.

Women of the Empire

Throughout all levels of society, the Incas saw men and women as complementing each other. Indeed, in some activities, both sexes took an active role. While men cleared and plowed fields, for instance, women planted the crops. Some mining crews were also made up equally of males and females.

Although most Incas traced their descent from their father's side of the family, members of some groups in the empire did so from their mother's. There were even Incas who simultaneously traced a woman back through her mother's family and a man through his father's.

Still, most women lacked power within Incan society. Yet there were some who had larger social responsibilities. A few women controlled land and herds, and others were religious leaders, priestesses of the moon god and other female deities. Moreover, empresses often swayed their husband's thinking, thus influencing imperial policies indirectly. Some even played a more active role. The wife of fifteenth-century emperor Pachacuti Inca Yupanqui, for instance, ruled Cuzco when he was away, even supervising disaster relief after a particularly violent earthquake. Similarly, the empress of Pachacuti's son, Topa Inca Yupanqui, concluded a treaty with the city of Yanayacu, a rival Andean state.

The Household

The basic social unit of the Inca Empire for all classes was the household, or family. Indeed, family structure was much the same for emperor, aristocrat, or commoner. And it was groups of related families that formed the local community in which most Incas lived, no matter their class.

The head of each household was male. The remaining family members were the man's wife or wives and his children. A wife was expected to serve her husband in whatever ways he thought fit. This expectation applied to all women, regardless of their social rank. The same expectation applied to children until they married and moved in to their own home.

Under Incan law, whereas women could have only one husband, a man could have more than one wife, but only if he could afford it. Typically, only the aristocrats could afford this luxury. Even those men who had multiple wives had just one principal, or official, wife. The others were deemed secondary wives. Only the principal wife was wed in a ceremony; the secondary wives were merely brought in to the household. The Sapa Inca had many wives, but as was customary, he too had only one official wife, the *coya*, or empress.

Incan society did not permit divorce between a husband and his official wife. A man,

Royal Display

In his *History of the Inca Empire,* the seventeenth-century Jesuit Bernabe Cobo paints a picture of the privileged life of the Incan emperors.

"The Incas [emperors] made a majestic display both in their personal style of life and adornment and in the pomp and splendor that accompanied them and with which they were served inside and outside their homes.... They were served all the exquisite, precious, and rare things that the land produced....

The king ate while seated on a small stool.... The table was the ground, as it was for the rest of the Indians, but it was set with great... richness, including... sumptuous [lavish] food.... Serving women brought him all his food on gold, silver, and pottery plates and set them before him on some very thin, small green rushes [reeds]. When he pointed out the dish that he wanted,... one of the... women would take it to him and hold it in her hand while he ate.... All leftovers from the meal and whatever the Inca touched with his hands were kept by the Indians in... chests...; thus in one chest they kept the little rushes...; in another, the bones of the poultry and meat left over from his meals.... Everything... was kept in a... [hut] that an important Indian had charge of, and on a certain day each year it was all burned.

Wherever he went,... the Inca was carried on the shoulders of bearers supporting a splendid litter.... When the Inca traveled, he had a large following.... The Inca also showed his majesty by traveling slowly..., and wherever he stopped, accommodations [lodgings] were prepared for him as elaborately as if he were in his court."

however, could tell a secondary wife to leave at any time. She, on the other hand, could not leave him.

The *Ayllu*

Households were collected together into groups called *ayllus,* the Quechua word for ancestors. The number of households in an *ayllu* varied, but its members were at least distantly related, the men and many of the women being descended from one or more common ancestors. Archaeologist Michael E. Moseley observes:

> Common ancestors gave ayllus their ethnic identity, and... [leaders] ruled by claiming close blood-ties to founding forefathers. Ayllus were often named after their founders, who were heroic figures, if not mythical ones, and could turn into stone or some special object. They secured lands for their people, established codes of behavior, and were models for proper life.[9]

Each *ayllu* was divided into upper and lower halves, or moieties. Members of the upper moiety claimed the closest ties to the founding ancestor, while those of the lower were more distantly related.

An *ayllu* had its own political and religious leaders, who oversaw the group's affairs and conducted *ayllu* ceremonies. Individuals served first in political offices and then in religious ones before retiring from public life. The senior political leaders of each moiety were joint rulers of the entire *ayllu.* In practice, one of the two was the senior partner; the senior partner was not necessarily the upper moiety leader.

Members of an *ayllu* lived together as neighbors, either in a town or in a farming community. Each division of an *ayllu* controlled its own section of the community. Depending on the size of the *ayllu*, each community section might be further subdivided.

A Spanish illustration depicts each of the fourteen Incan emperors. The Incas continued to revere their emperors long after their death.

An Ordered World

Royal *Ayllus*

The emperor's household was its own *ayllu* and a large one at that since Incan rulers always had many wives and children. In addition to the reigning monarch's *ayllu*, the royal *ayllus* of all previous emperors remained active. When an Incan monarch died, his body was mummified, and he was treated as though he were still alive and an active member of the *ayllu*. According to historian María Rostworowski de Diez Canseco, each of these royal *ayllus*, known as *panaca*, "had the obligation to preserve the mummy of the deceased ruler and guard the memory of his life and achievements by means of songs . . . and paintings passed from generation to generation."[10]

As was usual for nonroyal *ayllus*, all of a dead emperor's male and female descendants remained members of his *ayllu*, with one exception. That exception was the current Inca, who created a new *ayllu* for himself and his household.

Upper and Lower Cuzco

When the Spanish arrived in Peru in 1532, there were eleven *panacas*. Five of these royal *ayllus* belonged to a larger division called the Hanan Cuzco (Upper Cuzco) and six to the Hurin Cuzco (Lower Cuzco). As the names imply, each cluster of royal *ayllus* inhabited its own half of the city of Cuzco.

The *panacas* in the Hanan Cuzco belonged to the most recent Inca rulers, while those in the Hurin were the *ayllus* of older leaders. Because the Hanan contained the *panacas* of the four emperors responsible for the expansion of the Inca

The Second Emperor

In 1964 scholar R. Tom Zuidema proposed that the Incas did not have one emperor but two who were corulers. Terence N. D'Altroy examines this possibility in his book *The Incas*.

"A number of scholars support Zuidema's proposition that Inca government may have been a diarchy [a dual emperorship]. . . . That is, there were always two Inca kings, one from Upper Cuzco and one from Lower Cuzco. His proposal starts from the observation that Andean social organization, including Cuzco's, featured opposing halves, each of which had its own leader. Several [Spanish] chroniclers also wrote that Manqo Qhapaq [Manco Capac, the legendary first Incan ruler] was considered to be the founder of both social divisions. Without taking the latter premise at face value, Zuidema infers that the names of *panaqa* [*panaca*] may have been titles for groups holding a particular status, not the names of kindreds [related individuals] in a historical genealogy. . . . If Zuidema is correct, then we cannot assume that each *panaqa* corresponded neatly to a generation. . . . Although the . . . diarchy models are influential, they remain a minority viewpoint because they require elevating individuals to the Inca king lists who are virtually, if not altogether, absent from most lists of Inca royalty cited in the chronicles. In addition, Lower Cuzco almost certainly had a paramount figure [a leader], but studies of kin-based political systems throughout the Andes show that the leader of one social division invariably stood higher in rank than the other and spoke for the group as a whole in external relations and in . . . decision-making."

Empire, it was the more powerful of the two groups.

Imperial Succession

The imperial heir was always a member of the Sapa Inca's *ayllu*. However, unlike a European ruler whose firstborn, legitimate son or daughter was automatically heir to the throne, the Inca emperor might choose any one of the sons of his official wife as heir, not necessarily the oldest. The Incan emperor selected the son he thought most capable of ruling the empire. The sixteenth-century Spanish chronicler Pedro de Cieza de León writes,

> The Incas had no clear line of succession; they were like the Romans. . . . The Roman Caesars invariably looked for a suitable successor, . . . trained, and enthroned him. The Inca descended through the male line, but without fixed rule; i.e., the eldest son did not automatically inherit unless he proved himself worthy. The selection of the Inca-to-be was approved by the Inca's council of elders.[11]

In theory, sons of the emperor's secondary wives were barred from succession. However, sometimes such sons seized the imperial title by force, as did the last Incan emperor, Atahuallpa.

The imperial heir often underwent a trial period in which he shared the imperial duties with his father. If the designated heir failed to perform well or lost favor for some other reason, he would be replaced by another son. This practice was a source of friction among the potential heirs and often led to palace intrigues and civil war upon an emperor's death.

In a way, the entire Inca Empire that the imperial successor inherited was a large *ayllu* at the head of which was the emperor. In theory, all the men in the domain were the Sapa Inca's sons and all the women, his wives. And in a very real sense, the emperor owned almost everything and had authority over everyone in the empire.

An Ordered World

CHAPTER 2
Bureaucrats and Taxpayers

The ordered Incan society was important in the empire's ability to keep its economy healthy. Each social class—emperor, aristocrat, and commoner—had its duties and its obligations. To ensure that these obligations were met, commands and authority flowed from the top (the Sapa Inca), through the layers of bureaucrats (members of the nobility), and down to the common people. This tight management led to a well-controlled economy and the empire's wealth.

Incan Economy

The Incas had a moneyless economy: They had no coins or any other form of currency. Instead, they had what scholars call reciprocity; that is, goods were exchanged for work or vice versa. When the emperor wished to reward an imperial official or an army officer for serving the empire, he gave them jewelry, fine textiles, weapons, livestock, land, and even women to be secondary wives. Commoners, working on government projects, received food and clothing as a reward for their labor.

Three valuable resources, land, livestock, and labor, formed the foundation of the imperial economy. Scholar María Rostworowski de Diez Canseco observes that "the yield created through the exploitation of these resources was translated into consumable goods, which were stored in warehouses and represented the state's assets."[12] Among these consumable goods were clothing, food, tools, and weapons.

Owning the Land

Private land ownership was rare in the Inca Empire. In the Cuzco Valley, some Incas-by-privilege owned farms and country estates. Most land in the empire, however, belonged to the royal *ayllus*. By custom, the *panaca* of a former emperor retained ownership of all the dead ruler's land and the wealth it produced. The living Inca, therefore, had no access to the property of the former emperors. This custom forced a new ruler to quickly find means of supporting his *ayllu*. Some scholars speculate that this need for income may have been partially responsible for the expansion of the Inca state, with each new monarch adding new lands in order to build his own treasury.

The *panacas* allowed much of their land to be used by others. Each *panaca* divided its territory into thirds. In this way, part of the land was reserved for the Incan state, part for various temples, and part for the local *ayllus*. Those sections of land reserved for the use of temple and *ayllu* could not be sold or traded.

Ayllu Land Management

Each *ayllu* parceled out its land among its households, with every household head being assigned a tract that was large enough to support him and

Life Among the Inca

his family. Archaeologist Louis Baudin notes that these tracts were not equal in size:

> Each family received . . . a plot of ground which should be sufficient for sustaining life. . . . This plot varied according to the quality of the soil, which is logical. With the birth of each son a supplementary [extra] plot was allocated [given] to the parent, and with the birth of each daughter a half plot.[13]

Along with the parcels came control of water sources—such as springs, lakes, and even rivers—that were needed to raise crops on the land. Irrigation canals were also part of the land gift, and their maintenance was the responsibility of those using them.

Storing the Surplus

A portion of the crops from the emperor's fields was used to feed the imperial household, but much of the harvest was placed in imperial storehouses. Clothing and many other ordinary things were also stashed in these warehouses. Even more exotic items, such as dried birds, were stored as well. Sixteenth-century Spanish writer Pedro de Cieza de León reported that the Inca had

> great storehouses filled with all necessary supplies. This was to provide for their soldiers, for in one of these storehouses there were lances, and in another, darts, and in others, sandals. . . . Likewise, certain

Today, Spanish colonial buildings line the streets of Cuzco. In Incan times, enormous storehouses were the most conspicuous feature of Cuzco and other cities.

buildings were filled with fine clothing, others, with coarser garments, and others with food and every kind of victuals [food supplies]. When the lord [the emperor] was lodged in his dwellings and his soldiers garrisoned there, nothing, from the most important to the most trifling, but could not be provided.[14]

The stored items were used for far more than the emperor's pleasure or supplying the imperial army. They were given as gifts, as emergency rations in times of famine, or to people who had lost all their possessions in house fires, earthquakes, or floods. They also were available to anyone who was too ill, too old, or too disabled to work.

The Storehouses

The empire had thousands of storehouses filled with food and goods, representing much of the realm's wealth. Each major Incan city had from five hundred to two thousand such warehouses, which were built in rows along nearby hillsides. The elevation protected the contents from getting wet from flooding, but it also served as a grand display to the local people of the wealth and power of the Incas. The storehouses were also spaced sufficiently far apart to keep fire from spreading easily from one to another.

Built of stone and with several thousand cubic feet of storage, the warehouses were either circular or rectangular in shape. Instead

Imperial Storehouses

The Inca Empire had thousands of storehouses filled with food and goods, which represented much of the realm's wealth. Archaeologists Craig Morris and Donald E. Thompson studied the remains of these structures at the provincial Incan city of Huánuco Pampa. Their findings are revealed in their book *Huánuco Pampa: An Inca City and Its Hinterlands*.

"Long lines of storehouses overlook Huánuco Pampa from a hill to the south. Approaching the city on the Inca road from Quito to Cajamarca . . . one can see the warehouses from more than 30 km [18 miles] before actually reaching the city, announcing the wealth of the [Sapa] Inca and the security of his installation. . . .

The state warehouses of the Inca, at least in the Peruvian central highlands, have three . . . characteristics. Instead of regular doors with a threshold at ground surface, they have one or more window-like openings. They are normally placed in rows on a hillside above any residential structures that may be associated with them. And, finally, in the excavated sample that had . . . pottery [in it], that pottery was overwhelmingly large, narrow-neck jars. . . .

The warehouses take two forms, rectangular and circular. The windows of the circular face uphill. The rectangular [storehouses] . . . of the top row and the third row from the top have a single room. Those of the second and fourth rows from the top are usually divided into two rooms. . . . Only two structures have more than two rooms. . . .

The storage of maize . . . seems to be limited to circular structures. . . . Not all circular structures were reserved for maize. While only root crops [potatoes] were identified in rectangular [warehouses] . . . , the sample is so small that we cannot conclude that rectangular storehouses were devoted . . . to tubers."

of a door, each had one or two openings, much like windows, just above ground level. The interiors of the storehouses were either a single or a double room. The floors were often covered with gravel, and goods were placed in narrow-neck ceramic jars on the floor.

Mining and Herding

In addition to agricultural fields, land that contained mineral wealth was also valuable. Gold, silver, and copper were much prized for making tools and jewelry. In general, the emperor did not share mining real estate with others. Nevertheless, Spanish accounts indicate that some mines northeast of Lake Titicaca were set aside for use by the local population.

Livestock was also a part of Incan wealth. The Incas kept vast herds of llamas and alpacas (relatives of the camel), as well as some other domestic animals, on parcels of farmland. Such livestock was valuable because animals provided meat and wool. As with land, private ownership of livestock did not exist, except for the *panacas* and some Incas-by-privilege. However, nonroyal *ayllus* and state temples had the use of many of these animals.

Barter

Although householders did not own their own land or livestock, they did own whatever crops were raised on the land, as well as any clothing, pottery, or tools that they made. Commoner households were allowed to trade any excess food and goods they produced for other types of food, clothing, tools, or cookware. Without money, all trade was barter, and bargaining dominated since no set value for anything existed. For instance, trading corn for a ceramic cooking pot required the respective owners to bargain until they agreed on a fair trade.

Incan communities had no central place for the trading of food and goods. Of the Incan city of Huánuco Pampa, archaeologists Craig Morris and Donald E. Thompson report, "No major spaces were given over to market style exchange. Products of the fields . . . were exchanged instead among people related by kinship or political ties, and . . . these exchanges do not appear to have involved gathering at some common marketplace."[15]

Though the Incas did not have marketplaces, they did have fairs. Every nine days, commoners gathered in the central square of the nearest city or town to listen to proclamations issued by the emperor. At this time, they may have taken the opportunity to trade among themselves.

Imperial Trade

In addition to local trade, some trade between regions of the empire existed. However, this type of trade was the monopoly of the emperor. It consisted entirely of luxuries for the aristocracy: fine textiles, gold and silver jewelry and figurines, and elaborately designed ceramic pots and statues. Part of this luxury trade was coca, which was made by crushing up dried leaves of the coca plant and mixing them with lime. Incas chewed this product as a protection against fatigue and cold. The emperor himself normally had a bag of coca hanging from his waist.

Pack trains of llamas or human bearers carried these luxury trade goods throughout the empire—and even into the territories of neighboring peoples not yet a part of the Incan state. Along the coast, fourteen- to twenty-foot-long

Traders working for the emperor dealt in luxury items such as this solid gold figurine wrapped in a multicolored textile blanket.

rafts, made from balsa logs lashed together and powered by a single triangular sail, were the chief means of transporting trade items. In fact, the first European contact with the Incas was the capture of one of these rafts by a Spanish ship in 1527.

Labor Tax

The empire might have lacked money, but it still had taxes. In this society without machines, human labor was so important in getting work done that people paid taxes in the form of labor or other services to the empire. One such tax was the *mit'a*. To pay the *mit'a*, each commoner household sent one of its male members to work for the imperial government. The *mit'a* was due every year, and its period of service varied from a few days to a few months.

Mit'a workers built cities and roads. They carved out of the sides of mountains flat, walled terraces that provided level ground for growing crops. They worked in the mines and car-

Life Among the Inca

ried crops from the fields to the storehouses. They served in the homes of the nobles. And they soldiered in the army. While serving at these tasks, the men were clothed and fed out of the imperial storehouses.

In general, at any one time only about 3 percent of any *ayllu*'s households had a member on *mit'a* duty. Usually, the other members of the household could work around the missing man, and from time to time, they could always call on assistance from other close relatives. On the rare occasions when a large draft of men was needed from a single community or when the work period extended into a year or more, the labor of the missing was often replaced by other *mit'a* workers.

Working the Fields

Another labor obligation of the commoners was the agricultural tax, which required householders to help plant, tend, and harvest the crops and tend the herds that belonged to the emperor and to the temples.

Women were exempt from the *mit'a*. However, once a year, the women of each household had to make at least one woven garment that went into the empire's warehouses. They, as well as their children, also worked alongside the men performing the required labor in the fields. In a 1560 report the Spanish official Polo de Ondegardo noted that "all the inhabitants went forth except the aged and

To create arable land in the Andes, the Incan emperor forced commoners to carve level, walled terraces like these out of mountainsides.

infirm, dressed in their best clothes, and singing songs appropriate for the occasion." As with *mit'a* workers, Ondegardo adds, "when the people worked upon them [the imperial and temple lands], they ate and drank at the cost of the Inca."[16]

Working Aristocracy

The Incan aristocracy was exempt from all imperial taxes. But however rich and exempt they might be, these nobles were not idle. They served at the highest levels of the imperial government advising the emperor, carrying out imperial decisions, and acting as judges. They also served as the generals and senior officers of the empire's army. In addition, members of the nobility formed the priesthood.

Helping the Incan aristocracy in these duties were officials called *curacas*, non-Incas who made up the third highest tier of Incan society. The *curacas* were either local leaders of a subject people or recruits from those folk with a gift for management. They formed a secondary aristocracy, and received some of the same privileges as the Incan nobility. The *curacas* took care of day-to-day administrative tasks in their local areas.

Emperor and Prefects

The exact process of imperial decision making is not known. Even the size of the imperial government is unknown. Nonetheless, scholars do know that general policy was made by the emperor in consultation with senior advisers. These advisers were prefects, or *apos*. Headquartered in Cuzco, the *apos* were well-seasoned, experienced government officials. They were all relatives of the Sapa Inca.

Each *apo* was in charge of one of the four major divisions, or quarters, of the empire. All of these divisions began at Cuzco and radiated out, making the empire look like a pie sliced into quarters. In area, the sections were not equal in size. To the north was Chinchaysuyu and to the south, Collasuyu, the two largest divisions. The considerably smaller segments were Antisuyu and Cuntisuyu, to the east and west, respectively. It was the job of each prefect to see that the emperor's orders were carried out in his division of the empire.

Provincial Governors

The four quarters of the empire were further divided into some eighty provinces. Each province roughly equaled one conquered realm. Some of the larger conquests occupied more than one province, while some of the smaller were lumped together, making for provinces of about the same size.

In charge of each province was a provincial governor, known as the *tocricoc apo*. Like the *apos*, *tocricoc apos* were Incan nobles, often members of the royal family. Provincial governors had two major responsibilities: They enforced imperial law, and they looked after the interests of the people of their province.

Each governor was housed, along with his staff and other imperial officials, in a provincial capital that served as an administrative center. It was here that the barracks for *mit'a* workers were located and that various artisans, such as those who produced pottery or gold and silver objects, had their workshops. These centers also served as gathering places for major religious ceremonies. According to scholars Craig Morris and Adriana von Hagen:

28 Life Among the Inca

The Second-Most Powerful Inca

Writing in the late 1500s to the king of Spain, Huamán Poma, a descendant of a high-ranking Incan official, describes the second highest ranking Inca after the emperor. Poma calls this man a viceroy, but he was in fact a prefect, or *apo*—the emperor's chief adviser and a close relative (a brother or an uncle) of the emperor. Poma claimed to be descended from such an official. His description is found in *Letter to a King: A Picture-History of the Inca Civilization*.

"The Viceroy, who was called *Incap rantin*, was second only to the Inca.... He was never of humble birth and neither wealth nor wisdom had anything to do with his authority. His position derived solely from his descent from an ancient dynasty of Kings [emperors]. Lesser chiefs . . . were not entrusted with such a high office.

He was the person with whom the Inca usually dined, drank, amused himself and held conversations. Being the next in power he was also sent on important missions to Chile or Ecuador. His rank and lineage procured obedience from even the greatest of the nobility, who would have rebelled against any lesser person. As Viceroy and Captain-General [commander-in-chief of the army] . . . , he held authority under the Inca in all of Tahuantinsuyu from the last mountains of Chile to the northern sea and from the jungles of the Amazon to the sandy beaches of the Pacific Ocean."

Their architecture, and usually their pottery and other portable artifacts, immediately identify the centers as . . . [different from] the local system of towns and villages. They counted members of the ruling elite from Cuzco among their population. . . . Most of the people who used . . . [their] facilities . . . came for relatively short periods to pay their labor tax while living as guests of the Inka [Inca], whose storehouses provided for them during their stay.[17]

The *Curacas*

A single province was home to 20,000 households or families. The imperial government split these families into two sections of 10,000 apiece. Each section was further subdivided into two clusters of 5,000 households. The division continued through groups of 1,000 households, 500, and finally 100.

Administration of these different-sized household units was in the hands of the *curacas*. Two senior officials oversaw each of the ten thousand–household sections, while *curacas* of lesser rank supervised each of the smaller units. The *curacas* were the ones who made sure that the correct number of people showed up to work on imperial projects, such as road or building construction. They also supervised the collection and transportation of harvested crops and other goods to storage facilities.

The provincial governor rewarded *curacas* who did their jobs well. Senior *curacas* could expect gifts of servants or land and livestock from the emperor himself. A *curaca* who did a poor job, on the other hand, was punished by the provincial governor. If the *curaca* was judged lazy or incompetent, he was publicly reprimanded and dismissed.

Bureaucrats and Taxpayers

Imperial Law

In the Inca Empire, those guilty of crimes often faced torture and death. Jesuit clergyman Bernabe Cobo in his 1653 *History of the Inca Empire* provides a summary of Incan law, a code that favored the nobility over the commoners and men over women.

"He that killed another to rob him received the death penalty, and before it was executed, the guilty person was tortured. . . .

If someone was killed in a quarrel, first it was determined who caused it; if the dead man did, the killer was given a light punishment . . . ; if the one who caused the fight was the slayer, he received the death penalty, or at the very best, he was exiled . . . [to] serve for his whole life in the Inca's . . . coca fields. . . .

The husband that killed his wife for adultery was set free without punishment, but if he killed her due to anger . . . , he received the death penalty if he was an ordinary man, but if he was an important gentleman [aristocrat] . . . , he did not die, but he was given another punishment.

The woman that killed her husband received the death penalty. . . . She was hung up by the feet in some public place, and she was left like that until she died. . . .

In certain cases marriage was prohibited, and fornication [sexual relations] in the cases in which marriage was prohibited was punishable with the death penalty, if the guilty party was not a noble, because a noble got only a public reprimand. . . .

He that robbed without reason, besides paying for the stolen item if he had the resources, was exiled. . . .

He that stole things to eat from necessity was reprimanded and given no other punishment."

If he was dishonest or cruel, he was executed.

Arrest and Trial

Major officials at all levels of the Incan government acted as judges, depending on the nature of the case. Minor disputes, such as fights between husbands and wives or arguments between neighbors, were brought before the local *curaca*. He listened to the complaints of the parties involved and then rendered a judgment.

More weighty matters, such as theft, rape, and murder, were passed on to the provincial governor, who alone in a province had the power of life and death. The accused was brought to the provincial capital and kept in jail until the trial. A corps of constables existed to carry out arrests. The sixteenth-century writer Huamán Poma, himself a descendant of a high-ranking imperial official, observed that these constables "carried as their symbol of office a bag or pouch of the type used for carrying coca leaves; and they also wore sandals similar to the Inca's own. In this way their warrant was recognized and respected in the whole of our country."[18]

On the day of the trial, both accused and accuser presented their cases to the provincial governor. Witnesses might also be heard. After the testimony, the governor decided then and there whether the accused was innocent or guilty. If innocent, the accused was freed. If the verdict was guilty, punishment followed quickly, often as soon as the trial was over.

Punishment

Punishment was often harsh. Torture and execution were common sentences for everything from adultery to burning down government buildings. Another typical punishment was to drop a heavy stone onto the shoulders of the wrongdoer. The goal of this rock-dropping punishment was to inflict pain but not to injure or kill.

Other punishments were just as painful but more lethal. Adultery often resulted in the guilty parties being hung up by the hair until they died. And some crimes, such as treason or practicing black magic, called for the entire family of the convicted to be clubbed or stoned to death. This was done on the theory that no one could practice these acts without his immediate relatives knowing it.

This ceremonial wooden goblet bears the likeness of an Incan nobleman. The nobility served as imperial advisers, military officers, and priests.

Bureaucrats and Taxpayers

Not everyone was equal under the law. A crime that would earn a commoner death would merit an aristocrat a public scolding. The Incas believed that such a public humiliation for a noble was sufficient punishment. The only times the elite were executed were when they committed treason or in some other way displeased the Sapa Inca.

Language

Whether handing out judgments or work assignments, Incan officials had to be able to communicate with the people under them. Indeed, the Incan government could function only if its many people and parts could talk to one another. That demanded a single language. Therefore, the Incas required *curacas* to master Quechua and ordered that commoners teach their children the language.

However, the empire did not insist that people give up their native speech. And for a time, many of the realm's inhabitants were bilingual. The constant use of Quechua, though, generally eclipsed most native languages. Later, the Spanish would find Quechua as worthwhile as the Incas had in communicating with their Andean subjects and would continue its use.

Keeping Local Ways

The Incas allowed their subjects to keep more than their original languages. Indeed, the emperor and imperial officials found it to their advantage to leave local customs and religions alone as much as possible. The Incas commanded that each conquered people take its place in Incan society and that its members participate in Incan state religious ceremonies. But otherwise the subjects were allowed to keep their own dress, their own gods, their own coming-of-age rites, and so on.

Accordingly, any concessions that did not undercut Incan authority or lessen the efficiency of the workforce were granted to imperial subjects. This policy of tolerance reduced resentment toward Incan rule.

Resettlement

The tolerance policy, however, did not interfere with the Incas' need for control. As historian Rebecca Stone-Miller writes, the Incas "captured foreign leaders, artisans, and religious icons [ancestral mummies and other sacred relics] . . . and held them hostage in Cuzco."[19] Such actions were designed to guarantee obedience to the empire, whose needs came before all else.

Sometimes those needs demanded great sacrifices from commoners. When the Incas added territory to the empire, wrote Ondegardo in his 1560 report, "they caused the natives, who had previously been widely scattered, to live in communities."[20] Such resettlement could require far more drastic relocation. For example, if a province lacked enough people to work all its productive land, imperial officials forced families from more densely populated provinces to leave their homes and migrate to the place that needed workers. If the local population increased sufficiently, the transported workers eventually returned home. Otherwise, their move was permanent.

Troublemakers

The Incas also used resettlement as a way of dealing with rebellion. Troublemaking groups would find themselves far from their homes, living in unknown territory, and generally surrounded by loyal Incan subjects. Still other loyal households were then ordered to move to the rebels' original homeland.

The Incas required the relocated troublemakers to keep their native dress. This practice ensured that the resettled could not easily integrate with their new neighbors and thus would remain isolated and under the watch of officials.

In general, however, the bulk of the imperial population was obedient, choosing to live quietly under the emperor's rule. For most people, the empire was simply the backdrop against which their personal lives played out.

CHAPTER 3

Private Life

The Incas did not measure an individual's life in years but in stages of life. The entrance into each phase of life involved rituals, celebrations, and obligations. Infancy was the first stage, and childhood the second. The final stage was adulthood, which brought with it marriage and the responsibilities of setting up and running a household.

Comfort, particularly physical, was not an important part of an Inca's passing through these phases of life. Incas prepared themselves for a life of work and duty.

Infancy

Even birth did not call for pampering of either the expectant mother or the newborn. Incas made almost no prebirth preparations other than the expectant mother praying for an easy delivery. Usually, the mother continued working until the baby came.

There were no physicians or midwives among the Incas to help at birth; rather, the immediate family and close relatives provided aid. Indeed, some women gave birth without any assistance. During delivery, the father fasted. If the woman delivered twins or a child with a birth defect, she and her family fasted and prayed since such a birth was considered a bad omen.

For a normal birth, the mother's first act after delivery was to wash the baby in cold water and then wrap it in a cloth. The cold bath was the first step in a toughening process that would continue throughout childhood.

Commoner wives were expected to return to housework almost immediately after delivery. They carried their babies strapped to a board on their backs while they worked.

Naming Ceremony

Incan children received a childhood name when they were one to two years old. Later, at puberty, they were given an adult name. For the first naming ceremony, relatives and family friends gathered, with each cutting a lock of hair from the child's head and presenting a gift. The senior male member of the family finished the barbering and also cut the child's nails. The hair and nails were saved. All classes gave clothing as gifts, and aristocrats offered gold and silver jewelry, weapons, and livestock.

The ceremony ended with a feast and dancing that, for important Incan families, lasted up to four days. Dancing for the Incas was always linked to some specific celebration and was never a social activity in and of itself. The dances were formalized, with steps and moves that each partner followed.

Childhood

Incan children did not play a great deal. Indeed, according to the sixteenth-century Spanish writer Garcilaso de la Vega, who was part Inca, from infancy onward the Incas:

brought up their children . . . , rich and poor, without distinction, with the least possible pampering. . . . Every morning . . . [the infant] was washed in cold water, and often exposed to the night air or dew. . . . It was said that this accustomed babies to cold and hardship, and also it strengthened their limbs. . . . The mothers never took the babies into their arms or on their laps. . . . They said it made them crybabies.[21]

Nevertheless, children did enjoy some leisure activities. They occasionally played with balls. Tops were also a favorite toy and were spun by being flicked with a whip. Children played games as well, though their rules are no longer known. One game involved small, round pieces of pottery.

In general, young Incas had little time for these games, however, for as soon as they were old enough, they began helping their parents. Boys guarded animals and chased birds and other pests out of planted fields. Girls looked after newborns, sewed, cleaned, and cooked.

Usually, fathers supervised boys, and mothers looked after girls. The only exception was

An Incan mother, along with her daughter, sells goods at a market in this 1950s photo. At a young age Incan children help their parents, abandoning play for work.

in aristocratic households, in which each son of the principal wife was given one of the secondary wives as his nanny. The woman bathed and cared for the boy until he reached puberty. At puberty, she taught him about sex, and when he married, she went with him to his new home.

Education

Among the Incas, there was little formal education, all of which was reserved for aristocratic boys. The imperial position on education for commoners was summed up by one Incan ruler, who said, "It is not right that the children of the plebeians [commoners] should be taught knowledge . . . , lest the lower classes rise up and grow arrogant and bring down the public [empire]: it is enough that they learn the trades of their fathers."[22]

Parents provided most of a child's necessary education. Fathers taught their sons how to make tools, weapons, and shoes, while mothers instructed their daughters in practical domestic matters.

Both husbands and wives taught their children to know their place in society and instructed them about their obligations to the emperor and the empire. For commoner families, the imperial inspectors determined how well the children learned these teachings.

Schooling

The sons of the elite, meanwhile, were given four years of schooling at the House of Teach-

---

Incan Knowledge

Incan education for aristocratic boys consisted in part of mathematics, geography, and music. Garcilaso de la Vega, the seventeenth-century chronicler who was himself part Incan, explains in his *The Incas: The Royal Commentaries* what the Incas understood about these subjects.

"[The Incas] knew a great deal of geometry because this was necessary for measuring their lands, and adjusting the boundaries and dividing them. But this was physical knowledge, obtained with strings and stones used for counting and dividing, and nothing to do with heights [measured] in degrees. . . .

In geography they were able to depict, and each tribe could model and draw its towns and provinces as they had seen them. They did not trouble about other provinces. Their skill in this was extreme. I saw the model of Cuzco and part of the surrounding area in clay, pebbles, and sticks. It was done to scale with the [city] squares, large and small; the streets, broad and narrow; the districts and houses, even the most obscure; and the three streams that flow through the city, marvelously executed. The countryside with high hills and low flats and ravines, rivers and streams with their twists and turns were all wonderfully rendered, and the best cosmographer [geographer] in the world could not have done it better. . . .

They knew a great deal of arithmetic. . . .

In music they understood certain modes, which . . . [they] played on . . . reed pipes. Four or five reeds were bound side by side, each a little higher than the last, like organ pipes. . . . One gave the low notes, another higher, and the other higher still, like the four natural voices: treble, tenor, contralto, and bass."

ing in Cuzco. Beginning around the age of twelve, young nobles attended lessons in religion, history, geometry, astronomy, language, poetry, and music. They would repeat back the lessons to their teachers, who maintained discipline by applying ten strokes of a rod across the bottom of the feet. Such beatings were limited to one per day.

In addition, aristocratic boys spent time training to be warriors. They ran races and fought mock battles. Competition was fierce, and some participants were seriously injured in these fights.

Coming of Age for Boys

At age fourteen, Incan boys underwent puberty rites that officially marked them as men. At this time, they received their adult names, which were often the names of admired animals, such as Poma (Mountain Lion), Amaru (Snake), and Uturunku (Jaguar). Anthropologist John H. Rowe notes, "A man might be named for his father or grandfather. . . . He might acquire a nickname such as 'weeper of blood' . . . [or] 'stone-eye.'"[23]

Aristocratic boys had to undergo a series of tests of strength, endurance, and courage. After religious ceremonies, the boys raced each other to the top of a nearby hill, showed their skill with slings and bows, and fought each other in staged war games. Then, they had to stand sentry duty for several nights in a row without sleep. Next, they silently bore hard punches to the shoulders and remained still without flinching while an army officer swung a club above and alongside their heads. The officer then threatened their eyes with a spear. Finally, each young man made a bow, a sling, and a pair of sandals.

In the final ceremony the emperor pierced the young nobles' ears with a gold pin and gave each a set of gold ear disks. They then received a loincloth, the mark of manhood among the Incas. Upon returning to Cuzco, relatives gave the young men gifts (which often included weapons) and lectures on how they should conduct themselves in the service of the emperor. To maintain the harsh lesson of the rites, each gift was accompanied by the stroke of a whip.

For commoner boys, there was no testing of skills or bravery. Instead, in a public ceremony at the nearest town, they were given their loincloths and their names. As scholar Michael A. Malpass points out, "the special ceremony for noble boys indicates the importance of becoming a warrior . . . in Incan society. No doubt the rituals also served to create special bonds between the participants."[24]

Coming of Age for Girls

Puberty rites for girls, both commoner and aristocratic, were private and held in the home. Childhood for young women ended with the first menstruation. At that time, each girl fasted for three days, after which she was allowed on the final day to eat a little raw corn. Her mother then bathed her, braided her hair, and dressed her in new clothing.

Following this was a two-day feast, which her relatives attended and at which she served the guests. At the feast the girl received presents and an adult name. Women tended to be named after admired qualities, such as Ocllo, meaning "purity," or for beautiful objects such as a star (Cuyllor) or gold (Qori). The name was given to the young woman by her most important male relative, who also advised her to serve and to obey her parents.

Private Life

Entering Adulthood

Boys of the Incan nobility had to undergo a series of trials before being judged adults. The Spanish chronicler Garcilaso de la Vega, whose mother was Incan, describes some of these rites of passages in his 1616 book *The Incas: The Royal Commentaries*.

"The candidates were required to observe a very strict fast for six days, receiving only a handful of raw *sara* (their corn) apiece and a jug of plain water.... Such a rigorous fast was not usually permitted for more than three days, but this period was doubled..., in order to show if ... [the candidates could] suffer any hunger or thirst which they might be exposed to in time of war.... Anyone who showed weakness ... or asked for more food ... failed.... After the fast they were allowed some victuals [food] ... and then ... made to run from the hill called Huanacauri ... to the city, ... a distance of ... a league and a half [five miles].... Whoever reached [the finish] ... first was elected captain over the rest. Those who arrived second ... and down to tenth fastest were also held in great honor, while those who flagged [faltered] or fainted ... were disgraced and eliminated....

The next day they were divided into two equal bands. One group was bidden to remain in [a fort] ... while the other sallied forth [left]. They were required to fight ..., the second group to conquer the fort and the first defending it. After fighting ... for the whole day, they changed sides on the morrow [the next day].... In such struggles the weapons were blunted ...; nevertheless there were ... casualties which were sometimes fatal, for the will to win excited them to the point of killing one another."

Marriage

Marriage followed these puberty rites by a decade for men and about half that for women. Men generally married at twenty-five and women between sixteen and twenty. Normally, marriage partners came from within the same *ayllu*. Members of the upper moiety were generally required to marry those from the lower and vice versa. For commoners, bride and groom could not come from the same household or even be close relatives. They could be no closer than fourth cousins.

Different rules applied to the emperor and the Incan aristocracy. Prior to the late 1400s, the Sapa Inca traditionally married a princess of another Andean state, thus forming a political alliance through marriage. However, beginning with the emperor Topa Inca Yupanqui (1471–1493), the Inca leader married one of his full sisters, that is, a sibling with whom he shared the same mother and father. This incestuous relationship symbolically created a link between the current emperor and Manco Capac, the legendary first ruler of the Incas. Manco supposedly married his sister, thus beginning the royal line.

Like the emperor, an aristocratic groom could choose one of his father's daughters. Unlike the emperor, however, he could only marry a half-sister. So, although the bride had the same father, she had a different mother.

Incest, as practiced by the Incan emperors and nobility, eventually produces children with below-normal intelligence, as well as other mental and physical problems. However, since such incestuous marriages were a custom for only a short time among the Incas, these problems had yet to appear at the time of the Spanish Conquest in 1532. At least, no record of them exists.

Wedding Ceremony

The Incan wedding ceremony was relatively simple, even for the aristocracy. The bride and groom first obtained the approval of an Incan official, always the emperor for Incas-by-blood and Incas-by-privilege. Next, the bride returned to her parents' home, at which time the groom and his family arrived. Then, to show his acceptance of her, the young man placed a sandal on her right foot and grasped the bride's hand.

Both families then went to the house of the groom's parents. There, the new wife presented her husband with a fine woolen shirt she had made. Finally, after a period of lectures to the newlyweds on how to be proper spouses, the families joined the rest of the *ayllu* for a wedding feast.

Imperial marriages were much more elaborate. For instance, at the wedding of Emperor Huayana Capac (1493–1527), the bride and groom, each accompanied by a procession of high officials, met in the main temple in Cuzco. Outside the city, fifty thousand warriors stood guard. At the temple, the Incan high priest married the royal couple. Days of feasting and dancing followed.

An eighteenth-century engraving depicts an imperial Incan wedding, with its large procession of high-ranking officials.

Some areas of the empire had different marriage customs. In some places, for instance, to seal the marriage, the groom brought firewood and did other work for the bride's parents.

Housing

After the wedding, the newlyweds moved in to a house that had been built for them. If they were commoners, fellow *ayllu* members did the building. Aristocrats used *mit'a* labor to construct their new homes. The couple's relatives supplied them with cooking utensils and other necessities to furnish the home.

The average commoner and minor aristocratic house was a one-story rectangular building made from stone blocks and sometimes coated with adobe, a sunbaked clay. There was usually a single door that was centered in one wall but no windows. The steep roof was made of thatch.

Three or more houses were grouped together in a compound. In the center of the compound was a patio, which was often unpaved. The entire compound was generally surrounded by a wall.

Palaces and Estates

The emperor and the most important of the Incan nobility had palaces. Like other housing, the Inca palace was made of stone and was one story high. However, it had many rooms as well as interior courtyards and a few windows. The sixteenth-century missionary Martin de Murúa left this description of one of the imperial palaces in Cuzco:

> The great palace has two principal doorways, one at the main entrance and the other further inside. . . . At the entrance to the first doorway there were 2,000 Indian soldiers, on guard. . . . At the second doorway was the armoury. . . . Further on, there was . . . [a] large court or patio for the palace officials or servants, and still further, there were the rooms . . . where the Inca lived. This was full of delights because there were many kinds of trees and gardens and the dwellings were very spacious and . . . adorned with much gold and carved engravings of the figures and exploits of the Inca's ancestors. . . . At intervals there were niches and windows worked with silver and inset with precious stones.[25]

The palaces were located either in Cuzco or on large estates in the country surrounding the Incan capital. These estates were farms or retreats where the owner could get away from the affairs of the empire. Many of them were actually small cities in themselves, with buildings to house the owner's family and servants, private fields to supply food, and religious shrines for worship.

Inside the Home

Inside most Incan homes was a single room with a dirt floor. There were no decorations or engravings on the walls. Niches carved into the walls served as shelves and cupboards. Between the niches were stone pegs for hanging blankets and tools. A small clay, wood-burning oven was built into one end of the room. It was used for cooking as well as to heat the house. Extra food and spare clothing were stored in jars on the floor.

The Incas generally did not have furniture. The only exceptions were small stools that were used by important members of an *ayllu* and stone benches found in some country estates. For sitting, the Incas used blankets.

Ruins of an Incan palace in Machu Picchu reveal its many rooms, windows, and courtyards.

At night, the entire family would wrap themselves in their blankets and sleep at the end of the room opposite the oven. Not having nightclothes, they slept in the same clothes they wore during the day.

Bathing and Sanitation

Commoner houses had no baths or toilet facilities. Bathing was done in nearby rivers and streams. In the warmer parts of the empire, commoners bathed year-round, but in the colder Andean highlands, few bathed in the winter.

Sanitation needs were attended to in a niche built into the outside of the house. Privacy was nonexistent and the odor ignored. The household would collect the solid waste and use it to fertilize its fields.

The palaces, on the other hand, had both bathtubs and indoor latrines. Channels or copper pipes supplied both hot and cold water to

The Weavers

Among the Incas, one of the most important duties of married women—aristocrats or commoners—was weaving. The part-Incan author Garcilaso de la Vega details this domestic chore in his 1616 book *The Incas: The Royal Commentaries*.

"[Incan women] busied themselves with spinning and weaving wool in the cold districts and cotton in the hot. Each woman spun and wove for herself, and for her husband and children. They sewed very little for the garments worn by both sexes required very little sewing.... Every piece of cloth that they made ... was made with four selvages [borders]. Cloth was never woven longer than was needed for a single blanket or tunic [shirt]. Each garment was not cut but made in a piece, as the cloth came from the loom....

The Indian women were so fond of spinning and so reluctant to waste even a short time that as they came or went from the villages to the city or even one quarter [house] to another, visiting one another . . . , they carried equipment for the two operations of spinning and twisting [threads of yarn together]. As they walked along, they twisted what they had spun, this being the easier task. While visiting they would take out their distaff [wool-holding rod] and spin as they conversed. Spinning and twisting on the road was done by the common people, but ... [those] of the royal blood were accompanied by servants carrying their yarn and distaffs. Thus both the callers and ladies of the house were occupied and not idle while they conversed.... The quantity that they spin is little, because the operation is a lengthy and complicated one."

---

the tubs, which were made of tight-fitting masonry. The emperor and the aristocracy bathed frequently, at least once a day when possible. The toilet area in the palaces was a semiprivate cubicle with walls but no door. It had a channel in the floor through which water flowed, carrying off the waste.

Housekeeping

Whether in the home of a noble or a commoner, the role of men around the house was limited to making footwear and tools. Although aristocrats sometimes did these chores themselves, in general they had servants, or *yanaconas* to perform such tasks. Incan men, instead, spent their time working outside the house (commoners performing *mit'a* and other labor, and nobles concerning themselves with government work).

Among the commoners, wives were responsible for all the other housekeeping tasks: cooking, cleaning, and making their family's clothing, for which they did all the spinning, weaving, and sewing themselves. Imperial inspectors made regular visits to check on the conditions of each commoner household. They were interested in seeing how clean a house was and how sanitary the food preparation.

According to Malpass, royal and noble women had a much easier life:

The lives of noble women were no doubt easier than those of commoners; they had yanaconas [servants] to tend to many of the duties assigned to women. Yet fundamental activities such as spinning and weaving were conducted by all women, of high class or low. Principal wives were in charge of running the household and delegating duties to the secondary wives. Their task was more managerial: making sure that the household ran smoothly and that food and drink were prepared to high standards when important individuals were entertained. It probably fell to the secondary wives to do the preparations.[26]

Meals

The Incas ate twice a day, at 8 or 9 o'clock in the morning and 4 or 5 in the afternoon. Cookware consisted of ceramic pots that sat on tripods or pedestals. The household women would prepare soups and stews in the pots and then place them on their supports directly over the fire in the oven. Meat was impaled on sticks and roasted over the open flames.

A common food was a stew called *motepatasca,* made from corn, chili peppers, and herbs. Another was *locro,* a mix of meat, potatoes, peppers, and other vegetables. Popcorn was a special treat.

The Incas' favorite drink was *chicha,* or corn beer. To make it, Inca women chewed corn kernels, along with various seeds and fruits. They then spit the resulting pulp into a jar, which they let sit for several days. Their saliva caused the mixture to ferment. The longer the *chicha* sat, the stronger it was. The sixteenth-century Spanish chronicler Juan de Betanzos wrote that good manners required that,

> If a nobleman or noblewoman goes to another's house . . . , the visitor has to carry . . . a jug of *chicha.* On arriving at the house . . .

Weaving in Incan culture has both a practical and social significance. Incan women would talk and even walk with each other while making clothes and blankets.

they are visiting, they have two tumblers of *chicha* filled, one goes to the man being visited and the other to the man or woman giving out the *chicha*. . . . The one being visited does the same, also bringing out two tumblers of *chicha,* giving one to the visitor and drinking the other himself. . . . It is the greatest honor they can show each other.[27]

ate sitting back to back with the women, who faced the serving dishes. A wife filled her husband's plate and cup and then refilled them at his command.

For feasts, diners ate on the patio of one of the *ayllu* leaders, forming two lines facing each other. Those in each line were members of the same moiety. The most important person in each line sat on a stool at the head of his moiety.

Dining

Food was served on plates of pottery for the commoners and plates of silver and gold for the aristocrats. Tall cups made of wood, ceramic, or precious metal held the drinks.

At meals, Incas of all classes sat on the ground of the central patio. Aristocrats sometimes spread out a blanket on which food was placed. The men

Clothing

Besides cooking, Incan women made all the clothes for their families. They created the cloth by weaving cotton and wool yarn on looms. Each loom had two sticks, between which ran parallel lines of yarn. With wooden tools, the weavers threaded other yarn at right angles through these lines.

The clothing itself was simple in design. Women wrapped their bodies in a large piece

The Emperor's Pleasures

In the late 1500s, Huamán Poma, descended from Incan aristocrats, gave the following report to the Spanish king on what had entertained and diverted the emperor. This report appears in *Letter to a King: A Picture-History of the Inca Civilization.*

"Hunts were often made an occasion for feasts and pleasure. . . . The [emperor's country] estates were like immense gardens in which the animals ran wild for the pleasure of the ruler. . . .

A sure source of entertainment were the clowns and jesters, some of whom specialized in verbal foolery. There were also actors. . . . All of them contributed with their jokes and tricks to the amusements of these occasions. . . .

The Inca occasionally disguised himself as a poor man and went out from the palace on foot in order to find out what was happening and to see how other people lived. . . .

Our rulers were undoubtedly responsible for the widespread custom of chewing coca. . . .

Specially delicious food was prepared for the Inca. He used to eat maize that was as white and soft as cotton, a delicate sort of potato, the meat of white llamas and rabbits, . . . and lots of fruit. These foods were reserved for his own use and ordinary mortals risked the death penalty if they touched them. . . .

At one of his palaces he had a courtyard full of monkeys, parrots, hawks, doves, thrushes and other birds of the Andes. . . . He had water-gardens with fountains and fishes, and other gardens with flowers."

of cloth that they tied with a cloth belt at the waist and pinned at the shoulder. From the shoulder, they hung a mantle, or cape, that was fastened in front by a pin called a *tupu*. The *tupus* of commoners were generally made of copper, while those of the nobility were silver or gold.

Men wore a loincloth that they wrapped around the waist and groin. Over their torsos, they wore a tunic made from two pieces of cloth sewn together with slits left for the head and arms. During winter, men added a cloak.

Both men and women wore sandals, generally made from woven plant fibers or tanned leather. Upper-class Incas added gold decorations. Both sexes also wore headdresses, and each ethnic group in the empire had its own unique design.

Textile Artistry

Incan society prized textiles even above gold and silver jewelry. With the finest cloth, weavers created elaborate designs. They used dyed threads to create geometric designs or the figures of animals and gods. They also painted the figures onto the cloth. Occasionally, they wove gold or silver threads into the fabric or sewed disks or small plates of both metals onto the cloth. The designs on the clothing were not simply decorative; they were insignia that identified the wearer's ethnic group and social class.

The most prized clothing—always reserved for the aristocracy—was covered in part or in whole with feathers. Sometimes the garment was constructed entirely out of feathers. The smallest feathers came from hummingbirds, the largest from parakeets. Warm orangish hues, purplish black, and chrome yellow were some of the most prominent colors seen on these feathered costumes.

Recreation

Breaks from these daily household chores were rare. The Incas did not have much leisure time. Their society was too work oriented, in part because of the empire's needs but also because it took a great deal of labor to wrest a living from the hard Andean environment.

Still, the Incas did have games and sports. They played a number of dice games, using a die with five sides instead of six. They also enjoyed a board game that used beans as playing pieces. Unfortunately, the rules for these games have not survived.

Many of these games involved gambling. The wagers were normally clothes or livestock. Among the aristocracy, however, entire estates were sometimes bet. In one instance, the emperor Topa Inca Yupanqui even wagered a whole province on a game of dice with his son. The emperor lost.

In addition, fairs were held every nine days to break the monotony of work. But perhaps the greatest sources of diversion for the Incas were the feasts and dancing that accompanied special occasions. In addition to family affairs, these activities were part of the major religious ceremonies of the empire.

CHAPTER 4

Priests and Worshippers

For the people of the Inca Empire, religion was an essential part of life. They lived surrounded by their gods, in a world of spirits and sacred places. Every enterprise, no matter how great or how small, called at least for prayer and often for more elaborate rites.

The Imperial Faiths

The most personal of religions for all people in the empire was that of the *ayllu*. Each *ayllu* had its own traditions, holy days, and religious leaders. Each also had its own sacred relics, the most important of which was the mummified body of the *ayllu*'s founder. If an enemy captured these relics, it could hold the *ayllu* hostage.

In addition to local traditions was the Incan state religion. The empire depended on religion to tie its people together. The Incas imposed their religion on conquered people, but as an overlay, not as a substitute, for local gods and beliefs. As archaeologist Louis Baudin observes, "The Incas showed respect for the beliefs of the nations they subdued."[28] Since Incan religion and other Andean faiths had the same cultural roots and thus many shared beliefs, tolerating other practices was not difficult for the Incas.

However, the empire needed its subjects to be members of the state religion, which was an important political tool. Through ritual and instruction, Incan priests promoted the idea that the Incas had the goodwill and protection of the gods and that their imperial expansion was a divine mission.

In no way does this practical use of religion mean that the Incas lacked conviction or religious fervor. Sincerity of belief made their claims of being on a divine mission stronger and more convincing.

The Creator

The Incan religion had many gods. Chief among these deities was Viracocha, who created the world and all the other gods. It was said that Viracocha made humanity in his own image and then brought light into the world when, after crafting them, he pulled the sun and the moon from an island in Lake Titicaca in the Andes.

Spanish descriptions of Viracocha's statues reveal the god posed with right arm raised and fist clenched, except for thumb and forefinger. In the temple at Cuzco, his statue was a solid-gold, four-foot-high figure of a young boy. The emperor Viracocha Inca was named after this creator god.

The Sun

Below Viracocha were three major gods: Inti, the sun god; Illapa, the thunder god; and Mama-Quilla, the moon god. These were the sky gods, and their importance rested in their

Life Among the Inca

control of light and rain, two elements that were crucial to farming.

Inti was the god of agriculture and was the most powerful of the three. In addition to crops, the sun god also produced gold, whose color was that of the sun. Indeed, to the Incas, gold nuggets were the tears of the sun. Thus, according to historian Constance Classen, "as such it [gold] was used for the creation of sacred models [statues]."[29] Inti himself was portrayed as a golden disk with rays projecting from the rim and a human face in the center.

The sun god was the patron of the Incas because he was supposedly the ancestor of the Sapa Inca, who called himself the "son of the sun." According to tradition, the emperor Pachacuti Inca Yupanqui had announced this link between Incan royalty and divinity in the fifteenth century after Inti came to him in a dream. As scholar Brian M. Fagan notes, "In time, the people came to believe they were

This stylized sculpture represents Viracocha, the most important Incan god, who created the world and all the other gods.

Priests and Worshippers

under Inti's protection, and that their leaders were descended from this deity."[30]

The divine nature of the Sapa Inca, and by extension the empire, was crucial support for the Incas' belief that they had the right to conquer and rule. The emperor's claim that he was part god made it easy for imperial officials to argue that the empire's economic and social policies were god inspired and god protected. Consequently, the empire could claim a god-given right to the labor of its subjects.

Sky and Earth

Illapa, the god of thunder, controlled the weather and the rain and was portrayed as a man in glowing clothes standing in the sky. In one hand was a club and in the other, a sling. Mama-Quilla, the third sky god, was always depicted as a woman. She had no specific powers but served as Inti's wife. Legend had it that when Viracocha created the moon, she was as bright as the sun. A jealous Inti threw ashes on her face, dimming her light.

A whole host of other gods occupied positions beneath the sky gods. Pacha-Mama, another female deity, was the earth god who made the fields fertile and who shook the ground with earthquakes. Mama-Cocha, the female sea god, was the source of all water—oceans, rivers, lakes, springs, and even irrigation water. Other gods oversaw livestock, among many other tasks. Each was identified with a specific star or constellation.

Spirit World

The Incas also believed that the world contained spirits. These spirits were often associated with places and objects, called *huacas*. Scholars are unsure whether *huacas* were spir-

Viracocha, the Creator

The Incas gave credit for the world's creation to Viracocha, whose story here is retold by the sixteenth-century Spanish writer Pedro Sarmiento de Gamboa and reprinted in Constance Classen's *Inca Cosmology and the Human Body*.

"Viracocha . . . created a dark world without sun, moon, or stars. . . . After he created the world he . . . created men in his likeness, as they are now. And they lived in the darkness.

Viracocha ordered these people to live in peace and to know and serve him. . . . However, the vices of pride and cupidity [greed] were born among them . . . , incurring his wrath, and he . . . cursed them.

Then some were turned into rocks and others into other forms. . . . Over everything he sent a flood. . . . He kept . . . [some] men . . . to serve him. . . .

After the flood was over and the Earth dry, Viracocha decided to repopulate the Earth, and in order to do it more perfectly, he decided to create . . . light. To do so he went . . . to a great lake, . . . and in this lake there is an island called Titicaca. . . . Viracocha went to this island and ordered the sun, moon, and stars to emerge and go to the sky to give light to the world. . . .

Viracocha . . . drew on some large stones all the nations he thought to create. This done, he ordered . . . [each of his] servants . . . to take a different route and call the . . . peoples and order them to come out [from beneath the ground], procreate [breed], and swell the Earth."

its themselves or merely the dwelling places of supernatural beings.

Among the *huacas* were temples, tombs, hills, bridges, fountains, springs, lakes, and rivers. Caves south of Cuzco from which Manco Capac and the Incas reportedly emerged were holy sites, as were some quarries. Amulets, or charms, were portable *huacas* that were worn as necklaces or bracelets.

Sacred Stones

The most common *huacas* were rocks, which have a long history (predating the Incas) as sacred objects in South America. In general, except for amulets, piles of stones generally marked *huacas*. Passersby would add a pebble or rock to a pile as a sign of respect.

According to Incan legend, the first ruler, Manco Capac, had laid out the boundaries of the Incan domain by throwing four stones toward the corners of the earth. Manco himself was said to have turned to stone and was supposedly carried by the Incas into many early battles. In addition to Manco Capac, two of his brothers turned to stone. One of these alleged hardened bodies sat atop a hill near Cuzco and was one of the most sacred spots in the empire.

This was not the only *huaca* near Cuzco. The Incan capital was surrounded by sacred rocks. Other sacred rocks were the stones that legend said had aided in the defense of Cuzco against the mid-fifteenth-century attack of the Chanca, neighbors and imperial rivals of the Incas. As the story goes, these stones turned into warriors who drove off the Chanca.

Afterlife

Included among the *huacas* were the mummified bodies of the dead, particularly of the former emperors. The Incas believed that the souls of the dead looked after their living descendants. To repay ancestors for this watchfulness, Incas seated the mummified corpses at feasts, where portions of food and beer were set out before them.

The souls did not live on earth. Rather, they went to an Incan heaven or hell. An individual who led a good life went to live with the sun, while one who was bad ended up living beneath the earth. All Incan nobility, no matter how they behaved, automatically merited a place in heaven. Commoners, meanwhile, had to earn the right, probably in part by being good, obedient subjects of the emperor. Afterlife with the sun was believed to be the same as life on earth, except there was always enough to eat and drink. In the hell below the earth, it was cold, and hunger was the norm.

The Temples

Every major Incan city had a temple. The Spanish would later call all these structures "sun temples." In reality, many of these buildings housed all the gods, not just Inti. However, only Viracocha, Inti, and Illapa were usually represented by statues or paintings in the temples.

In Cuzco was the great temple of Coricancha, which means "golden enclosure" in Quechua. The name came from the gold that decorated the temple's exterior and interior walls. Considered the center of both the empire and the world, the temple was actually a complex of buildings that opened onto a plaza. Surrounding the entire compound was a wall with a twelve-hundred-foot perimeter. The largest building was the main shrine. Its lofty stone walls (their exact height is unknown) had three doors and several windows. In addition to the gold on the walls, gold thread was interwoven in the thatch of the building's roof. The

The circular wall pictured here once protected Coricancha, the great temple at Cuzco. The Incas regarded the temple as the center of both the empire and the world.

smaller structures may have been storerooms or housing for priests.

Coricancha served as a model for most of the other major temples of the empire. However, the Incas also had a number of single-roomed temples. Some of these structures were dedicated to Viracocha, while others may have been for Inti.

Inside the Temples

The Incas did not worship inside their temples but, rather, outside of them, generally in a city's plaza or town square. One exception may have been the temple near the modern Peruvian city of San Pedro Cacha. It had a large open interior that may have been used for ceremonies.

Most temples, however, were simply storehouses for priestly garments and holy artifacts. They were also filled with gold and silver statues and beautiful textiles, testifying to the Incas' wealth and prestige. At Coricancha, Inti was represented by a huge disk of gold that was embedded with gems. Sitting on thrones of gold and facing this disk were life-sized carved images of the former emperors.

In another part of Coricancha was an artificial garden built to honor Inti's role as a giver of life. The garden contained sculpted corn plants made out of gold. The corn was very detailed, showing stalks and kernels. The garden soil from which the corn rose was also molded from solid gold. Next to this garden was a group of llamas and their young, surrounded by shepherds—all again crafted from gold.

Some of the royal mummies may also have been stashed in Coricancha. Others may have been housed in the palaces of their respective *panacas*.

Priesthood

The temples also served as the living quarters of the priests and priestesses. Both priests and priestesses were members of the Incan nobility. The men conducted services to the male gods and the women to the female. Each deity had its own set of clergy. Those that served Inti were the most respected and powerful priests.

Members of the priesthood had specialized duties. Some conducted religious ceremonies, others heard confession, and still others managed the fields that fed and clothed the clergy. The produce from the temple lands was used to feed priests, priestesses, and other temple attendants. Some of it was also used in religious rites.

A particularly honored priest was the diviner, one who foretells the future. In search of revelation, diviners cut themselves off from other people. The missionary Martin de Murúa wrote in 1590,

> The Incas had some . . . philosophers/diviners. . . . These went naked in the most isolated and gloomy regions . . . and walking alone in these uninhabited places, they

Coricancha, Cuzco's Temple of the Sun

The sixteenth-century Spaniard Pedro de Cieza de Léon in his chronicle *The Incas* gives a detailed description of Coricancha, the main temple at Cuzco. This temple, built in the mid–fifteenth century, was not a building but a compound that contained several buildings within its walls.

"[The temple] had many gates, and the gateways finely carved; halfway up the wall ran a stripe of gold. . . . The gateway and doors were covered with this metal. Inside there were four buildings, . . . and the walls [of each] inside and out were covered with gold. . . . There were two benches . . . , which the rising sun fell upon. . . . These benches were for the Lord-Incas [emperors], and if anyone else sat there, he was sentenced to death.

There were guards at the doors of these houses whose duty it was to watch over the virgins [Chosen Women], . . . the most beautiful . . . that could be found. They remained in the temples until they were old. . . .

Around this temple there were many small dwellings of Indians who were assigned to its service, and there was a fence inside which they put the white lambs [llamas], children and men to be sacrificed. . . .

The high priest . . . dwelt in the temple. . . . Within the temple there were more than thirty bins [made] of silver in which they stored the corn, and the contributions of many provinces were assigned to this temple. . . .

I make no mention of the silverwork, beads, golden feathers, and other things which if I were to describe them, would not be believed."

gave themselves to divination and philosophy without rest. From sunrise to sunset they constantly stared at the sun, no matter how bright it was, without moving their eyes, and they said that in the great shining wheel they saw great secrets. They spent all day on burning sands [of the coastal deserts] without feeling pain, and they also patiently bore the cold and snow [of the Andes]. They lived a very pure and simple life, . . . [surviving] on what the earth produced without being mistreated by tools.[31]

All priests, no matter what their specialty, began their training as young boys. Some candidates inherited their positions. Others entered the priesthood because they were blind or deaf or even because they were struck by lightning, all signs that they had been touched by the gods.

Nothing is known about the exact duties of priestesses beyond their serving the female gods. How they were selected and trained is also unknown.

The High Priest

The high priest, who was also the head priest of Inti, was a close relative of the Sapa Inca. In theory, the emperor was the head of the religion, just as he was the head of state. However, his religious duties were confined to officiating at only very important ceremonies. Day-to-day administration was left to the high priest.

Elected by the aristocracy for life, the high priest was one of the most powerful people in the Inca Empire. According to archaeologist Ann Kendall, he "was so revered that he competed in authority with the Sapa Inca. He had power over all . . . temples, to which he appointed priests."[32]

Virgins of the Sun

Besides the clergy, the temples were served by attendants, both men and women. The Virgins of the Sun were chief among these servants. They were the Chosen Women, the *acllas*, assigned to religious duty. Their responsibilities included making *chicha*, a drink that was used frequently in ceremonies; cooking food that was given in sacrifice to the gods; and weaving clothes for the priests, as well as for gifts to the gods.

The Chosen Women came from all social classes: the Cuzco nobility, the families of *curacas*, and the commoners. They were selected by an imperial official, who sought out pretty and good-natured nine- and ten-year-old girls.

The girls were trained either at Cuzco or at the nearest provincial administrative center. Here, as anthropologist George Bankes writes, they were "taught . . . religion and how to dye, spin and weave cotton and wool to a high standard. Their training also included cooking and making fine chicha."[33]

Aclla Service

At thirteen or fourteen, the trained *acllas* were presented to the emperor. The Sapa Inca chose a few of the young women to be his secondary wives, and others were given as gifts to favored nobles. Of the remaining Chosen Women, some went to serve in the temples, while others became the teachers of new *acllas*. Still others spent their lives making the many elaborate garments that the emperor and the Incan aristocracy wore. Many took up posts cooking and making *chicha* for the *mit'a* work gangs.

Even more than most people in the empire, the Chosen Women were tightly controlled. They had to perform whatever tasks were set for them.

The descendants of the Incas still drink chicha, *corn liquor once brewed by virgin priestesses, during ritual ceremonies.*

Protection

Except for those who became secondary wives, the Chosen Women were forbidden to marry or to have lovers. Indeed, their virginity was jealously guarded. As with Incan justice in general, punishment was harsh for *acllas* who took lovers. Both man and woman were hung up by the hair to die.

Because of these restrictions, the compounds that the Chosen Women inhabited had very limited access. These compounds, which could number up to fifty buildings, were surrounded by a tall wall. A single narrow opening in one wall led into a small courtyard. The only exit from the courtyard was a door into a small building. This building finally opened onto the compound's central patio. Thus, unwelcome visitors could easily be denied entry by just a few guards.

Despite this lack of freedom, the *acllas* were among the most respected members of

Incan Prayers

According to Louis Baudin in his *Daily Life in Peru Under the Last Incas*, the following were two popular Incan prayers. The first was probably addressed to Viracocha, the chief Incan god, while the second was aimed at Inti, the sun god, from whom the emperor claimed descent.

"O Creator! thou who art at the ends of the earth, thou who givest life and soul to men, and sayest to each man, 'Be thou such a kind of man,' and to each woman, 'Be thou such a kind of woman,' thou who, speaking thus, didst create and fashion them and didst give them life. Protect these men whom thou hast made, that they may live safe and sound, sheltered from danger, and in peace. Where art thou? In the highest heaven or in the depth of the thunder and the storm clouds? Hear thou, answer me, be kindly disposed towards me. Give us life eternal, hold us in thy hand, and receive this offering wherever thou mayst be, O Creator!"

"O Creator! May the subjects of the Inca [emperor], the peoples in subjugation to him, and his servants, rest in safety and peace in the reign of thy son, the Inca, whom thou has given us as king. Whilst his reign lasts, may thy people multiply and be kept safe, may it be for them an age of prosperity, may everything increase, fields, men, and beasts, and guide always with thy hand the monarch to whom thou has given birth, O Creator!"

---

the empire. Their roles in cloth production and as *mit'a* support staff made significant contributions to the Incan economy. Their service to the Incan temples also enhanced their reputation since the state religion was extremely important to the Incas and to the empire.

Ritual Offerings

Ceremony and the ritual that accompanied it were at the heart of Incan religion. Theology took a backseat, as Bankes observes:

> Inca religion was mainly concerned with ... ritual rather than mysticism and spirituality. Divination was regarded as important ... [before taking] any action. ... It was particularly important for the individual to ensure that the supernatural forces of the environment were kept in a benevolent mood, otherwise physical or economic misfortune might befall him.[34]

Sacrifice, offering something of value to a god, was an important part of almost every Incan ceremony. Just as goods were exchanged for service around the empire, they were offered in religious rites as payment for supernatural aid. Sometimes the sacrifice was food and coca, which would be burned, and *chicha*, which was poured on the ground. Fancy textiles, seashells, gold, and silver were also burned as offerings.

Animal Sacrifice

Live offerings were considered the most pleasing to the Incan deities. Among these sacrifices, llamas were a favorite among the Incas. Each major god had its particular color animal. For example, Viracocha received a brown llama; Inti, a white; and Illapa, a mixed color animal. After the priest cut the sacrificial llama's throat, he smeared its blood over the image of one of the gods, which was placed outside the temple for every ceremony.

Llamas were also used in prophesying the future. After killing the animal, priests removed the lungs and, wrote the Spanish missionary Christoval de Molina in the 1570s, "inflating the lungs, through a certain vein, discerned certain signs by which they declared what was about to happen."[35]

When an imperial heir was named, a priestly examination of a llama's intestines was undertaken. If the reading was favorable, the candidate was judged suitable to be emperor. If the signs were not favorable, he was supposedly rejected and a new heir named. To what extent this ceremony actually influenced imperial succession is not known.

Human Sacrifice

The Incas also practiced human sacrifice, the most valuable of all offerings. Such sacrifice was rare because it was reserved for very important events, such as the coronation or death of an emperor. Ceremonies in response to natural disasters and war also called for human sacrifice.

Most of the sacrificial victims were children between the ages of ten and fifteen because children were thought to be purer of spirit than adults. These children were always commoners. Boys were collected from households as another form of taxation. Girls came

This Spanish illustration inaccurately depicts an Incan human-sacrifice ritual. In reality, human sacrifice was rare, and most of the victims were children.

from the most beautiful of the commoner Virgins of the Sun.

According to archaeologist John Howland Rowe, "Selected boys and girls were . . . distributed for sacrifice to the major shrines [temples] of the realm."[36] Some even made months-long pilgrimages from province to province, where they were treated with great reverence. Being a sacrifice was considered a great honor among the Incas and the other Andean people, including the victims and their families. The sacrificed child was seen as being sent to live with the gods, indeed, to become a minor deity.

The Sacrifice

Before the sacrifice, there was a large feast, at which the children ate a last meal. This practice ensured that the victims would not go to the gods hungry. Often the children were unconscious by the feast's end from having drunk large amounts of *chicha* and were often killed before they could wake up.

Most of the children were sacrificed during ceremonies held in or near cities. A few sacrifices, however, took place atop some of the highest and—to the Incas—holiest of mountains, such as the Peruvian peaks of Pichu Pichu and the volcano Nevado Ampato. Priests took the children up to the summits of these peaks, where the victims were ritually killed and buried.

The method of death varied. Some children were struck on the head with a heavy club. Others were smothered or strangled. Still others had their throats cut or had their still-beating hearts torn from their chests. In a 1622 document, the Spanish official Rodrigo Hernández Principe reported on the fate of several Chosen Women:

> They [the Chosen Women] entered the plaza where the Inca was seated on his seat of gold together with the statues of the Sun, Lightning and Thunder, and the embalmed Incas and the priests who displayed them. . . . When the feast was over, . . . [the sacrifices] who were meant for Cuzco were taken . . . to the house of the Sun, . . . lowered into a vault, . . . and walled in alive. The others were sent back to their lands to have the same done to them.[37]

Dressing the Sacrifices

The sacrificed children were richly dressed. Their clothing could include elaborate feathered headdresses and shirts of fancy design normally reserved for the aristocracy. The shirts were often too large for the victim, who was apparently expected to continue growing in the afterlife.

Alongside the burial place of the slain victims were placed gold and silver figurines of llamas and people. The girls wore silver shawl pins and seashell necklaces.

Ceremony

The ceremonies surrounding the sacrifices on Pichu Pichu and Ampato were seen by very few, although large, well-attended rituals were probably conducted prior to the ascent of the mountains. Attendance at ceremonies likely varied according to the importance of the event. Of the regular ceremonies, those held in May, June, and December were the most important. In May, the Incas celebrated the corn harvest and in December the beginning of the rainy season. The festival in June was dedicated to Inti and only Incas-by-blood were permitted to participate.

In addition, the Incas held small daily ceremonies, most notably offering wood, cloth,

Harvest Celebration

The Incas had many religious festivals during the year. In May they celebrated the corn harvest, as the soldier Pedro de Cieza de León describes in his 1553 work *The Incas*.

"To celebrate this feast with greater devotion . . . , it is said that they fasted for ten to twelve days, refraining from eating much and sleeping with their women. . . . When this had been done, they . . . [had] large numbers of . . . llamas, pigeons, guinea pigs, and other birds and animals which were killed as sacrifice. . . . They anointed [covered] the statues and figures of their gods . . . with the blood, and the doors of the temples . . . , where they hung the entrails [intestines]; and after a time the soothsayers and oracles . . . [examined them] for signs. . . .

When the sacrifice had been made, the high priest and the other priests. . . . ordered the *mamaconas* [Chosen Women] to come forth richly attired and with a great quantity of . . . chicha . . . , serving it in goblets of gold from . . . tubs of silver. . . .

In the middle of the plaza they had erected . . . a great . . . [throne], covered with cloth of feathers thick with beads of gold, and great blankets of their finest wool, embroidered in gold and jewels. At the top of this throne, they placed the figure of . . . Viracocha, large and richly adorned. . . . And the Inca [emperor] with the nobles and the common people . . . , removing their sandals, . . . bending their backs and puffing out their cheeks, . . . blew their breath toward him. . . .

Below this throne there was the image of the sun . . . and that of the moon. . . . The statues of the dead Incas were brought out. . . . Many people . . . laid before them . . . little idols of gold, and llamas of gold, and figures of women, all small, and many other jewels."

and food to the sun. They also had special ceremonies to ask the gods' assistance with natural threats such as droughts and floods.

The Incas used two calendars to determine when these religious ceremonies should be held. One was based on the movement of the sun, the other on the moon. Besides marking religious observations, the solar calendar had some practical uses. The Incas employed it to decide when to plant crops and when to perform other agricultural activities, most of which were also associated with major religious celebrations. The lunar calendar apparently had only religious significance and was used to schedule important ceremonies dedicated to Mama-Quilla and to the various gods who were the stars.

The Rituals

The Incas prepared for major ceremonies by bathing and fasting. Fasting, which lasted from two to six days before the event, meant not eating meat, salt, chili peppers, and other spices and not drinking beer. The Incas also refrained from sexual activity during this period.

The ceremonial rituals varied. They often took place in the plazas of Incan cities or in nearby fields or hills. The priests sometimes brought out the images of Viracocha, Inti, and Illapa. In Cuzco, at such times, the royal mummies were also put on display. Priests offered sacrifices that occasionally required several hundred llamas. Many of these ceremonies ended with the burial of figures made from

The llama was the chief domestic animal of the Incas. Several hundred llamas at a time were sometimes sacrificed to the gods during religious ceremonies.

gold, silver, and seashells, plus the burning of carved wooden statues dressed in fine cloth. After the rituals were completed, the Incas danced, sang, ate, drank, and recounted high points of Incan history.

Death

There were no specific religious rites associated with either birth or death. However, there were rituals for the dead that were essentially the same for all social classes.

Funeral rites, which took place in the home, lasted from five to eight days. During that time, no fires were lit. The family of the dead person dressed the body in new clothes and then wrapped it in a shroud. In a final act of homage, the relatives, singing and weeping, circled the body in a slow dance to muffled drums.

Incas did not bury their dead. Instead, they put the bodies in small freestanding buildings. These buildings had room for more than one body, so entire families were eventually housed together. With the body were placed some of the deceased's prize possessions. All remaining objects were burned.

After the funeral followed several weeks or months of mourning, during which the surviving family members dressed in black and smeared black paint on their faces. If the deceased was a man, the women of the household cut their hair short and wore their capes over their heads. Indeed, a woman who dreamed of cutting her hair was thought to soon be a widow.

Imperial Death

The death of an emperor called for the same customs but on a much larger scale and with much more elaborate ritual. Mourners, some of them professionals, kept up a constant wailing in Cuzco and in other cities. Songs telling the story of the dead emperor's life were composed and sung. The deceased's favorite wives and servants were expected to volunteer to be strangled in order to join the Sapa Inca in death (the less willing were helped along).

Little is known about the method used to preserve the dead ruler's body, but part of the procedure required herbs that dried out the flesh and the removal of the intestines. The eyes were also removed and replaced with seashells designed to look like eyes. After mummification, the new emperor had the preserved body placed before the image of the sun god in the Cuzco temple, where people offered it sacrifices.

The mourning period after an emperor's death continued for a year, with poems and more songs being composed. Women all over the empire cut their hair. The new Sapa Inca arranged for large trains of pilgrims to visit all the important sites marking the dead leader's successes. To mark the end of mourning, people washed their faces with ashes to remove the pain of grief.

Even as they mourned, the people of the Inca Empire worked. They worked not necessarily to forget but because their labor was needed to keep the domain operating and because it was required of them.

CHAPTER 5

Working Life

The commoners of the Inca Empire experienced a life of toil. They supplied all the labor that was needed by the empire, and since the Incas had no machines, all that work was done by hand. The Andean region, as was true for the entire Western Hemisphere at the time, did not have large work animals. The llama, the largest domestic animal of the area, was able to carry only small burdens. It could not drag heavy loads or pull plows. Human muscle made up for the lack.

As for the aristocratic Incas, few of them, men or women, did much manual work. Servants attended to their fields and their houses.

A Harsh Land

The commoners' major task was farming, which for the Incas was a challenge. In the Andean highlands, many of the plateaus, such as the altiplano of Bolivia, are more than two miles above sea level. Even in the summer, night temperatures can drop below freezing. As scholar Michael E. Moseley notes, "Few crop types will grow at such heights."[38] In addition, frequent drought, hail, and heavier-than-usual frosts meant that good harvests came only once every three or four years.

Thus, highland farmers needed cold-resistant plants that could be stored for long periods of time. One of the main crops grown by the Incas was maize, or corn, which could be dried and stored for years. For storage, Incan farmers sometimes prepared harvested corn by boiling it to a soft paste or roasting it, or they might turn it into popcorn.

Potatoes were almost as important a food as corn. They were stored for long periods after alternately freezing and drying them. Imperial highland farmers also grew sweet potatoes, tomatoes, squash, beans, and chili peppers.

Lowland Farming

The coastal lowlands posed their own problems for farmers. The Pacific coast of South America is one of the driest regions on earth and has been for one hundred thousand years. Little rain falls in this land; some areas go as long as twenty years between rains. It is so dry that even low-water desert plants such as cactus cannot grow there.

A number of rivers, however, run through this arid land from the Andes to the sea, and their banks provide a home to strips of trees and plants. The rich river bottoms of the desert proved very good for raising beans, squash, peanuts, and corn.

Lowland farmers also grew a number of nonfood crops, of which cotton was the most valuable. Gourds, which when dried and hollowed out supplied vessels to carry and store water, were also prized. Farmers grew coca and tobacco there as well.

Planting the Crops

The growing season for the Incas began in August with planting and ended in March with the harvest (seasons in the Southern Hemisphere are reversed from those in the Northern). To know exactly when to start planting, the Incas had erected four towers outside Cuzco, two to the east and two to the west. From the city, the towers appeared to be on the horizon. In August, when the sun rose over the first tower in the east and set over the first tower in the west, it was time to plant corn and potatoes. When the sun rose and set between the two other towers a month later, it was time to plant the remaining crops.

At the beginning of each planting season, the Sapa Inca kicked off the work by making a small furrow in a field near Cuzco with a gold-tipped plow. Then, a number of high-ranking officials took brief turns at the plow. The emperor and his party quickly turned over the real work to the commoners and retired to a banquet prepared in their honor.

Working the Fields

According to archaeologist Terence D'Altroy, because of the conditions under which the Incas farmed, they "approached farming with weapons in their hands.... They envisioned agriculture as warfare—a victory claimed by disemboweling the earth."[39] Indeed, the prime tool Incan farmers used even looked like a weapon—a spear—as the

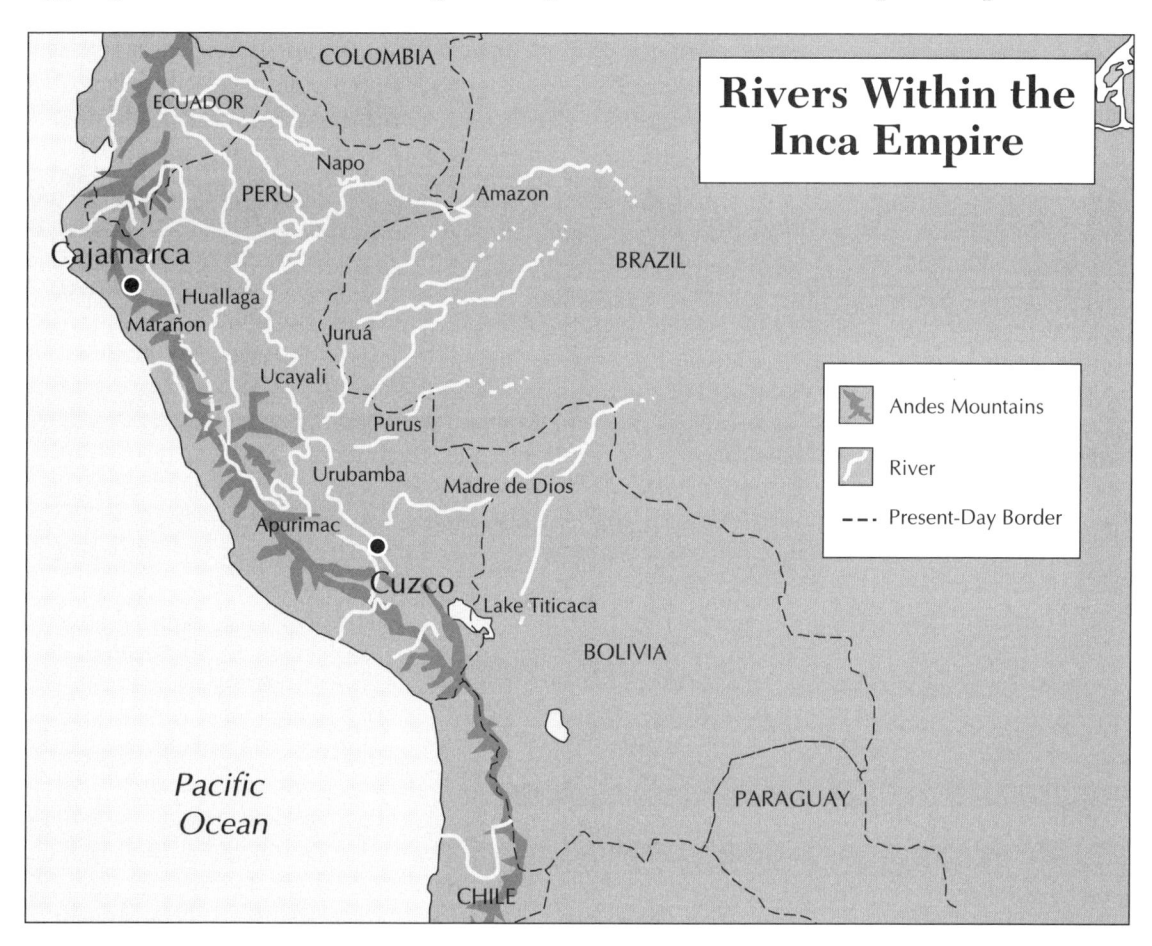

Rivers Within the Inca Empire

Working Life

following description by historian Edward P. Lanning reveals:

> An important Incan invention was the *taclla* or "foot plow," a long pole with a bronze point, a foot rest, and a handle. . . . It permitted the soil to be turned as with a plow rather than simply perforated [dug full of holes] for the planting of seeds. A line of men worked across the field, driving the *tacllas* in, turning up the soil, stepping back a pace, and repeating the process, while a line of women faced them breaking up clods with clubs or hoes.[40]

The work was hard, particularly if the soil was rocky.

The women also picked up any stones the plowing turned up. Their presence was needed not only for the work they did but also because the earth god, Pacha-Mama, was female. Thus, the Incas believed that women had a more intimate connection with the soil than men did.

Guinea Pigs and Llamas

Incan farmers also had domesticated animals. One of these animals was the guinea pig, which, although small, was the major source of meat throughout the empire. The most important livestock was the llama and its smaller cousin, the alpaca. Archaeologist Ann Kendall comments on the importance of these two animals:

> The llama was the only animal in the Andean region large enough to be used as a pack animal. . . . It could travel about 20 kilometers (12 miles) a day with a load up to 45 kg. (100 lb.). . . . Its wool was coarse but

Fertilizing the Fields

The sixteenth-century writer Garcilaso de la Vega in his *Royal Commentaries of the Incas and General History of Peru* left the following description of how Incan farmers fertilized their crops.

"They fertilized the soil by manuring it, and in the valley of Cuzco and almost all the highland area they treated their maize fields with human manure, which they regarded as the best. They go to great trouble to obtain it, and dry it and pulverize it in time for the sowing season. In the whole of [the province of] Collao . . . , the climate is too cold for growing maize, and they sow potatoes and other vegetables; for this they use the manure of the Peruvian sheep [llamas], which they regard as more beneficial than any other.

On the seacoast, . . . they use no other manure but the dung of sea birds, . . . which . . . [occur] in such enormous flocks that they seem incredible to anyone who has not seen them. . . . They deposit an amount of dung that is no less incredible. . . .

Each island [where the birds breed] was assigned, on the Inca's instructions, to a certain province. . . . Landmarks were set up to prevent the inhabitants of one province from trespassing in the area assigned to another, and a more detailed division was applied to each section, in which each village had its piece and each householder . . . his part. He was prohibited from taking dung from the area allotted to another village, for this was regarded as theft. . . .

In other parts of the same coast . . . , they manure with the heads of sardines and use nothing else."

could be used to make cloth-like sacks and plaited [woven] ropes. The alpacas, smaller animals with fine wool, . . . were kept primarily for their fleece. . . . All cameloids [llamas and alpacas] provided meat . . . and leather, as well as other commodities such as [dried] manure for burning.[41]

Herds of llamas and alpacas were prized possessions of the Incan emperor and his aristocracy. Although the emperor possessed the majority of the herds, he allowed individual households to have up to ten animals. All the livestock of an *ayllu* was normally herded together, with each family notching the ears or branding the flanks to mark its particular llamas or alpacas.

Hunting

Besides farming, the Incas also supplied their larders through hunting and fishing. In general, hunting was restricted to times when food was scarce—for example, when a bad harvest occurred or when disease had killed off numbers of domestic animals.

Each province of the empire had a hunting preserve in which the residents of that province could hunt. Like most land, the hunting grounds belonged to the emperor. Residents were therefore required to obtain a license to hunt there from the provincial governor.

Solitary hunting was not part of Incan culture. A group of sometimes thousands of commoners would form a large circle and then contract inward, driving deer and other Andean animals before them. When the animals were completely encircled, the hunters would kill them with stones from slings or other thrown weapons.

To capture birds, whose feathers were valued for headdresses and as decorations on clothing, hunters used a rectangular net slung

Like their Incan ancestors, these Bolivian fishermen use cigar-shaped reed boats to fish Lake Titicaca.

between two poles. The net was either dropped on birds before they took off or thrust up in the air to trap birds just taking flight.

Fishing

Fish was not an important source of food around Cuzco, where the lakes are few and the rivers too fast moving for fishing. However, farther south, at Lake Titicaca, the people lived mostly off fish, and after their conquest by the Incas, they supplied Cuzco with some fish.

Fishing was a very important source of food, however, along the coast. Here, fishermen set out to sea daily in small one-person boats. Each boat was made of reed and shaped like a cigar. There was no interior in which to ride. Instead, the fisherman straddled the craft

Working Life

with his legs while propelling himself with a paddle. These boat riders caught fish either with copper hooks or with nets that they strung between two of the boats.

Mining

In addition to their agricultural chores, commoners also served as the empire's miners. The Incas mined gold, silver, and copper. They used the first two exclusively for jewelry, utensils, and artwork. Copper also had its decorative uses. The *tupus* that pinned commoner women's cloaks were made of copper. This metal was also shaped into the priesthood's sacrificial knives.

By itself, copper is too soft to make usable tools. However, when mixed with either tin or arsenic, copper becomes bronze. Bronze is hard enough to make tools, and although the Incas appear to have used only a few bronze tools, they did make ax heads, chisels, knives, the heads of war clubs, and even tweezers out of this metal.

Working the Mines

Even more than farming, mining was a backbreaking task. Indeed, in recognition of the difficulty of this labor, the Incas required miners to work only from noon to sunset.

To reach copper, silver, and gold, miners dug shafts in the ground or drove them into mountain-rock faces, depending on where traces of metals were spotted. Digging was done by scraping the dirt away with wooden or bone trowels. To penetrate rock, miners heated the stone until it cracked. Then, they pushed wooden wedges into the cracks and, swinging stone hammers, drove the wedges deep until part of the rock face crumbled away. In this slow, laborious way, the miners dug tunnels that stretched almost 250 feet in length. The excavated dirt or rock, after being checked for silver and copper ore, was carried off in llama-hide sacks or baskets by other workers.

In addition to being hard work, mining was dangerous. Each shaft was only large enough for a single miner to enter. Cave-ins and bad ventilation often made working in the confined space deadly.

Not all mining required digging or wiggling into cramped shafts. A good amount of gold came from river- and streambeds. Miners removed gravel from a river or stream and washed it with water to reveal small nuggets of gold.

Tax Exempt

Some of the work that commoners did went toward paying their *mit'a* and agricultural taxes. However, some commoners did not have to pay these taxes because imperial policy allowed for tax exemptions for a number of professions.

One such tax-exempt group was the *yanaconas*, who formed a corps of permanent servants to the Incan aristocracy. The positions of the *yanaconas* were hereditary, with children following parents into service. This group's original members were rebels who had been sentenced to lifetime work in the houses and fields of the upper class. Although many of the *yanaconas* worked in lowly positions, some showed such talent for management that they were given government posts.

Not all household servants, however, belonged to the *yanacona* class. Many of the other servants of the nobility were fulfilling their *mit'a* duty, particularly those who worked for the *curacas*. Unlike the *yanaconas*, these *mit'a* servants worked in aristocratic households for

Life Among the Inca

Gold Mines

In his 1534 *An Account of the Conquest of Peru*, the Spanish soldier Pedro Sancho provides an eyewitness account of Incan mines and mining practices.

"The mines are in the gorge of a river about half-way up the sides. They are made like caves . . . whose mouths [were made by scraping] the earth . . . with the horns of deer and [the dirt] was then carried outside in certain hides sewn into the forms of sacks [of llama hide]. . . . The manner in which they wash the earth [to reveal gold] is, they take . . . water from the river, and on the bank they set up certain very smooth flagstones on which they throw water . . . and the water carries off the earth little by little so that the gold is left upon the flagstones. . . .

The mines go far into the earth. . . . A great mine which is called Huayna Capac goes into the earth some 80 meters [260 feet]. They [the mine shafts] have no light, nor are they broader than is necessary for one person to enter crouching down, and until the man who is in the mine comes out, no other can go in. . . . At night when they return to their houses in the village, they enter by a gate where the overseers . . . [receive] from each person . . . [the precious metal] that he has got. There are other mines . . . scattered about through the land, which are like wells, a man's height in depth, so that the worker can just throw the earth from below on top of the ground."

short periods of time and then returned to their homes.

Reading the Knots

Another set of professionals excused from taxes were the *quipucamayocs*, the imperial accountants. The Incas may have lacked writing, but they did have an accounting system. Imperial accounts told officials, for instance, how many households were in a particular area, how much corn was harvested and stored, or how large individual herds were.

The Incas recorded these accounts on the quipu, a collection of knotted, wool strings. Each quipu had a long, main cord, from which dangled different colored strings. Some quipus had hundreds of threads attached to the central cord.

Each string had a series of knots of different sizes. The size and position of the knots represented numbers. Those at the bottom (that is, farthest from the main cord) were 1 through 9. Knots in a string's middle were 10 through 99, and those at the top, 100 and above. In addition, the point from which a string hung from the main cord identified the item being tallied, such as corn, clothing, or even people.

A second type of quipu had geometric designs and other symbols tied to the strings. These were used to help people remember Incan history, songs, and poems. The symbols represented ideas or classes of events that made it easier to recall the full version of the stories as they were passed along orally.

The Accountants

It was the task of the *quipucamayocs* to read the quipus. Each *quipucamayoc* was a specialist. Some read only crop accounts, others preserved *mit'a* records, and still others kept military and religious accounts.

Incan merchants recorded transactions by means of the quipu, a device consisting of a series of knotted wool strings.

These quipu readers were scattered throughout the empire, living in cities, towns, and villages. Although a *quipucamayoc* worked closely with local *curacas*, he was answerable only to the provincial governor. As with other commoners exempt from the general labor tax, a *quipucamayoc*'s position was hereditary, and each accountant taught his son the knot code used in his record keeping. As the Spanish missionary Christoval de Molina remarked, in the 1570s, "The knowledge was handed down generation to generation so that the smallest thing was not forgotten."[42]

Litter Bearers

Another of the tax-exempt professions was that of litter bearer. A litter was a traveling device that consisted of a platform mounted on two parallel poles. On the platform was a stool for a rider. Sometimes overhead, there was a canopy for protection from the sun. Only the emperor and very privileged nobles could ride on litters.

Grabbing onto the poles, litter bearers hefted the litter up and carried it wherever its rider desired. Each litter required four men to hold it. The Spanish official Polo de Ondegardo reported in 1560 that "those who performed special services were exempted from other classes of tribute. There is an example of this in the province of Lucanas, where the people were trained to carry the litter of the Ynca [the Inca], and had the art of going with a very even and equal pace."[43]

Potters

Another group of tax-exempt commoners possessed such valuable skills that they worked only at a single profession. Among these professionals were the important artisans who worked in clay and metal. Of lesser importance were those craftspeople who worked in wood, bone, shell, feathers, and gourds.

Imperial officials set up whole communities of potters, even moving such workers from one province to another. This concentration allowed the officials to monitor the output of the potters and to ensure that their work conformed to standard designs, because pots were important measuring devices.

The most common storage container in the empire was a jar with a pointed bottom and a long narrow neck. Often used for storing and pouring *chicha* and other liquids, the jar's pointed base allowed it to be thrust into the

Life Among the Inca

ground, making it more difficult for someone to accidentally spill its contents. The container came in several different sizes, the largest being three feet high. The interior volume of each size jar was standardized, allowing them to be used in measuring out exact quantities of everything from corn to beer.

Potters, who appear to have all been men, did not have a potter's wheel and thus had to work the clay with their hands until it took on its final shape. For a jar, a potter made the body, neck, and handles separately. After assembling the parts, he painted the surface with a geometric pattern. The clay he used was mixed with chopped cornstalks to keep the piece from breaking while it dried in the sun or was fired in a kiln.

Metalworkers

Metalworkers, like potters, were prized artisans and also lived in their own communities. Each specialized in working a specific metal; the empire had goldsmiths, silversmiths, and coppersmiths. The first two concentrated on luxury items for the Incan nobility: bracelets, rings, necklaces, and other jewelry. Gold- and silversmiths also created small decorative figurines, some of which were dressed in headdresses and clothing. The coppersmiths, who worked in bronze as well as copper, made jewelry for the commoners, but they also manufactured more practical objects, such as metal tools, knives, and the tips of *tacllas*.

Metalworkers began by purifying the ore they received from the mines (except for gold, which naturally came in a pure state). To get silver and copper, the smiths had to crush the ore and then heat it hot enough to melt the metal out of the rock in which it was encased.

In what form the pure metal was then shaped is unknown. However, the Incan smiths worked it by hammering, welding, and casting to make the final product.

Silver Work

In his *Royal Commentaries of the Incas*, sixteenth-century chronicler Garcilaso de la Vega provides the following description of Incan silversmiths at work.

"They [silversmiths] never made anvils or iron or any other metal. . . . They used hard stones of a color between green and yellow as anvils. They planed and smoothed them against one another; and esteemed them highly since they were very rare. They could not make hammers with wooden handles. They worked with instruments [hammers] of copper and brass mixed together: they were shaped like dice with rounded corners. Some are as large as the hand can grip for heavy work; others are middle-sized, others small, and others elongated to hammer in a concave shape. They hold these hammers in the hand and strike with them like . . . stones. They had no files . . . nor bellows [for their furnaces]. . . . They [did not have] tongs for getting the metal out of the fire. They used rods of wood or copper, and thrust the metal onto a lump of wet clay they had near to temper its heat. There they pushed it and turned it over and over until it was cool enough to pick up. . . . They . . . realized . . . that smoke from any metal was bad for health, and thus made their foundries, large or small in the open air, in yards and spaces, and never under roof."

Artists

Although little is known about Incan artists—painters, musicians, and writers—they did exist. They were probably commoners, and some of them, at least the popular artists, may well have been exempt from the labor tax.

The Incas did not have painting aside from that found on their clothing and on their pottery. Whether the weavers and potters did their own painting is not known, but it is possible that artists separate from these professionals existed. In any case, as scholar Michael A. Malpass notes, the artists "used a relatively small number of decorative elements, especially triangles, feather patterns, and squares. Plants, flowers, llamas, pumas, and human figures were also used, although very often in a stylized and geometric manner."[44]

Musicians and Writers

Music was an important part of Incan life, and some of it was likely composed by professionals. Certainly, there were some full-time musicians, such as those who played for the Sapa Inca. They used a variety of instruments, including flutes, drums, seashell trumpets, tambourines, and bells.

The Incas also had literature, which was, of course, oral, and in many cases accompanied by music. The sixteenth-century chronicler Garcilaso de la Vega, part-Incan himself, remembered learning a love song as a boy:

> A love song in four lines occurs to me. It will show the style of composition and the concentrated and concise expression of what . . . [the Incas] wanted to say. Love poems were composed with short lines so that they could more easily be played on the flute. . . . The song is as follows:
>
> To this song
> Thou shalt sleep:
> In the middle of the night
> I shall come.[45]

In addition to poetry, Incan authors produced plays, prayers, and hymns. The dramas generally featured two actors and were performed as part of a dance at religious ceremonies. Some of the poetry was, like the above, love verse. Many poems, however, were narrative epics that recounted the myths, legends,

Love Poetry

Incan poetry was oral and meant to be accompanied by music. Among the most popular verse was love poetry, of which the following, reprinted in Terence N. D'Altroy's *The Incas*, is an example.

What evil Fortune separates us, queen! What barriers separate us, princess! My beautiful one, for you are a chinchiroma flower, In My head and my heart I would carry you. You are like the sparkling water, You are like a mirror of water, Why don't I meet my loved one? Your hypocrite mother causes our unbearable separation; Your contrary father causes our contrary state. Perhaps, queen, if the great lord God desires, We will meet again and God will bring us together. The memory of your laughing eyes makes me sicken. A little, noble lord, just a little! If you condemn me to weeping, have you no compassion? Weeping rivers, over the cantut lily, in every valley, I am waiting for you my little beauty.

and history of the Incas. Poems were always sung by the performer.

The names of the authors of these pieces have been lost. More than likely, since this literature was passed down verbally from generation to generation, many people actually had a hand in its composition, adding, subtracting, and altering as they saw fit.

Healers

One final class of workers, whose tax status is unknown, was medical practitioners. In general, the people of the empire believed that disease was the result of an angry spirit. The cure was to make some sacrifice—food or clothing—to appease the offended being.

In addition, Incans often treated pain by bloodletting. The individual would cut open a vein nearest the pain. For a headache, for instance, the preferred spot was between the eyes or the bridge of the nose.

For those who sought another method, there were the *hampi camayoc*, or medical specialists, who treated patients with herbs made from various plants. For instance, bark from the peppertree, a Peruvian evergreen, was boiled in water and was applied to fresh wounds. The root of the sarsaparilla plant, when boiled, was used as a pain reliever.

Medical practitioners in the Inca Empire also included surgeons. Surgeons treated patients complaining of internal pain. The surgeon drugged or hypnotized the sufferer and then cut open the person's stomach. He cleaned it out and at the same time pretended to remove snakes and toads. Incan surgeons also practiced brain surgery. Fluid sometimes collects inside the skull after head injuries and presses on the brain. To drain this liquid, surgeons either drilled holes in the skull or removed pieces of bone.

The head injuries that required such surgery were frequently suffered by soldiers who had been struck on the head in battle. Service in the imperial army was another way commoners paid their labor taxes.

CHAPTER 6

Army Life

For the Incas, the army was the chief tool for expanding the empire's borders. It was also an important safeguard against threats from outside and from within the imperial domains. Indeed, warfare was common among the Incas.

For those fulfilling their *mit'a* duty, serving in the army was the riskiest way of discharging their tax obligations. There was always the threat of being severely wounded or killed in battle. Plus, campaigns could stretch into years. The Sapa Inca Atahuallpa, for instance, before becoming emperor, led troops on a campaign against Ecuadorian rebels that lasted almost a decade. The rewards of a successful campaign, however, were great. Even common soldiers could expect to receive valuable cloth—if not more lavish presents—as gifts from a grateful emperor.

Organization of the Army

The smallest unit in the Incan army had ten soldiers under the leadership of a *chungacamayoc*, or a "guardian of ten," the equivalent of a modern-day sergeant. The *chungacamayoc* saw to it that his men were armed, supplied, and trained.

Five of these 10-man units were assembled under the command of a *pichca chungacamayoc*, or a guardian of 50, who supervised the unit leaders under him by making regular inspections. Increasingly larger army sections led to divisions of 100, 1000, 25,000, and 50,000 soldiers.

Guardians of ten and fifty were commoners, who, like their men, were fulfilling their *mit'a* obligation. Commanders above these ranks were *curacas* and Incan aristocrats, the latter often being career army officers. The highest-ranking general was the chief of the army and was chosen by the emperor and the imperial prefects. The chief was generally a brother or an uncle of the Sapa Inca but was always a relative of the royal family. The emperor, of course, was the head of the army, as he was both the head of the government and the head of the state religion.

Farmers and Warriors

Because the military was important to the Incas, fighting skills were prized attributes of Incan men. So, all able-bodied men began weapons training in boyhood. Undoubtedly, regular drills maintained these skills as adults—whether in war or peace.

The empire had very few troops on duty during peacetime. In fact, the only full-time soldiers were professional officers and the Sapa Inca's personal guard, an elite unit that numbered a few thousand men. Of the rest of the army, historian Nigel Davies notes, "the ordinary soldiers were . . . farmers who were liable for military service . . . , rather than warriors with no other occupation as in a modern standing army."[46]

Life Among the Inca

In addition to the small corps of professionals and the vast body of reserves, the empire had a group of semiregular soldiers. These latter troops garrisoned the fortresses that were placed throughout the empire and along its frontier. The forts generally sat atop hills overlooking cities and towns. Archaeologist Louis Baudin writes,

> These strongholds . . . allowed their occupants to endure a prolonged siege. They formed small townships, with houses and cultivated terraces, and they were self-supporting, at least for a certain length of time. . . . Their mission was to break the thrust of invaders and give the imperial armies time to mobilize. An invasion . . . from the eastern forests had miscarried [failed] against such defenses [in the early 1500s].[47]

The Fortress Folk

The inhabitants of these forts were full-time residents but not full-time soldiers. They and their families, who also resided in the forts, lived and farmed in the same way that commoners did all over the empire. They took up their weapons only when attacked.

These garrison folk were generally not native to the regions in which they served, particularly those at frontier posts. They were

Mountain Fortress

One of the largest Incan military posts was Pambamarca, located on a mountain about twenty miles northeast of Quito, Ecuador. Archaeologist John Hyslop in his book *Inka Settlement Planning* provides the following description of the remains of the complex.

"The highest and most central part of the Pambamarca complex is dominated by a massive installation . . . with five increasingly higher levels sustained [supported] by concentric walls. . . . The walls of this and other units are made of rough stone blocks quarried nearby. . . .

Many doorways are found in the concentric walls. . . . The remains of at least two dozen buildings [or units], all apparently rectangular, are found within the walls. . . .

Running just to the north of Unit 1 is a trench with two walls on either side. It connects Unit 1 with Units 6, 11, and probably 13.

[Unit 2] has three concentric walls. . . . There is no evidence of buildings. Unit 3 is lower and still simpler, with one concentric wall. The wall surrounds a rock outcrop [rock projecting from the ground]. Unit 4, the smallest in the complex, consists of only two concentric walls with no visible buildings. It rests directly north of an ancient road. . . . Units 4 and 5 may have controlled transit [travel on the road].

Unit 5 . . . is a massive installation. . . . Two outer walls at right angles indicate that it was probably rectangular. Outside of the main walls farther to the north there is a rock outcrop surrounded by three walls on the west and steep cliffs on the east. Two concentric walls . . . make up the . . . southern part of [Unit 5]. . . . There are several doors in the outer wall. . . . Traces of . . . eighty buildings are found in the center of the unit."

resettled loyalists with orders to make the forts their permanent homes.

The Coming of War

When war threatened, the imperial government put out a call to the provinces for enough *mit'a* commoners between the ages of twenty-five and fifty to fill military ranks. Each province sent to Cuzco, or to some other designated point, a body of troops under the command of a *curaca* general. The final assembled army usually numbered between 70,000 and 250,000 soldiers, depending on the nature of the crisis.

The Sapa Inca was always careful to avoid assembling too large an army near Cuzco. Its presence could prove too great a temptation for an ambitious army commander, who might use it to mount a coup and try to seize the throne.

Another concern in building an army was shortchanging the labor needs of each province. Because some crises could lead to lengthy wars, the empire planned for lengthy terms of military service—sometimes lasting years. Imperial officials often assigned other *mit'a* laborers to work the household land of soldiers on extended campaigns. As scholar María Rostworowski de Diez Canseco notes, "This [practice] permitted Inca armies to remain at the borders of the state for several consecutive years and meant that other men were made responsible for the crops and that their [the soldiers'] women remained in their *ayllus*."[48]

The Ceremonies of War

When the troops came together and waited for marching orders, they camped in tents outside their meeting point. They were carefully watched to see that they did not cause trouble. At the same time, they were well fed and given *chicha*. Entertainers sang for them to keep them amused.

Religious ceremonies were also a part of this waiting period, for Incan priests and sacred relics played a role in military events. Archaeologist John Hyslop explains:

> Many rituals were associated with military activities. . . . Rituals and divinations guided and accompanied almost every step taken before, during, and after a military campaign. Portable sacred objects were carried to war. Rites were performed and offerings made to strengthen the Inkas' efforts as well as to diminish those of the enemy.[49]

At the beginning of a war, the priests at Cuzco sacrificed wild birds and llamas before the "stone of war," a *huaca* that sat in the main plaza. The llamas had not been fed for days, and diviners examined the remains. If the dead animals' hearts had shrunk, it was a sign that the hearts of the enemy would grow weak and faint. Such ritual boosted the morale of Incan soldiers.

Setting Out

The marching order of the Incan army was by ethnic groups. The newest imperial subjects led the column. Those groups who had been in the empire longest, and were consequently considered the most trustworthy and loyal, were placed closest to the generals and the emperor, who brought up the rear.

The army was a colorful assemblage. Many warriors wore headdresses and their regional costume, decorating their shoulders and chest with feathers. Officers sported jewels and wore plumes on their helmets.

An Andean priest makes an offering at Machu Picchu. The Incas typically made ritual offerings both before and after battle.

There was no such thing as a standard military uniform. However, each squad of ten had a small, eight-inch banner with its own unique design that it carried fastened to a spear point.

The Long March

To reach the scene of battle required long marches, particularly to the frontiers, which were hundreds of miles, sometimes more than a thousand miles, from Cuzco. The march was guided by *rumancha*, or signalmen, who wore special insignia so that they could be easily recognized. Any soldier who broke ranks to steal food or threaten civilians was executed.

Common soldiers and most officers walked, while generals—and the emperor when he personally led the army—rode on litters. Four soldiers carried each litter, even into battle. Indeed, the emperor remained on his litter, surrounded by a thousand members of his bodyguard, throughout the entire contest.

Provisions for the advancing army came out of the state warehouses. While in the central provinces, the army was generally able to

Army Life 73

This nineteenth-century engraving depicts an Incan emperor as he offers clemency to conquered chieftains. The emperor usually executed chiefs captured in battle.

camp each night near towns and cities with storehouses. Here, food was distributed directly from storage to the troops. When the army reached the borderlands of the empire and beyond, supplies were carried to them by llama trains.

Ambassadors and Spies

Before an attack was launched, Incan ambassadors attempted to negotiate with the enemy. The sixteenth-century soldier Pedro de Cieza de Léon wrote of a campaign against a people known as the Wankas, "The captains of the Inka . . . [wanted] to win the graces of the Wankas without war and to have them go to Cuzco to recognize the king [emperor] as their lord; and thus, it is common knowledge that they sent messengers."[50] Sometimes, just the knowledge that a huge imperial force was bearing down on them was enough to persuade a defiant people to surrender and willingly join the empire. Moreover, the ambassadors were able to offer those who

74 Life Among the Inca

ceased resistance some privileges and assurances that their leaders would remain in place.

At the same time that the ambassadors were at work, spies slipped into enemy territory. Their mission was to discover the strength and position of the enemy army and to learn something about the land in which the Incas had to fight.

Battle Goals

When negotiation failed, battle quickly followed. The Incas' battle plans were straightforward. First, the soldiers were to capture the enemy's chief leaders and any of their foe's *huacas* that had been brought to the battlefield.

Accomplishing these goals depended largely on the Incas' overwhelming their opponents with sheer numbers. As soon as battle was joined, the conflict turned into a free-for-all of thousands of small hand-to-hand fights in which weapons skill counted but sheer numbers were even more important.

On the Battlefield

When the Incas finally confronted the enemy, they advanced to the accompaniment of drums, tambourines, and bone flutes. Trumpets made from clay or large seashells were used as signals. The warriors also sang and shouted. Sometimes, officers and men alike painted their faces to frighten the enemy. Both noise and paint were designed to unnerve the opposition.

The Inca high command sometimes divided the forces into thirds and then had one division attack the enemy while keeping the remaining warriors hidden. After fighting began, the other two units would rush in and attack their opponent's rear, or flanks. At other times, Incan generals hit an enemy's weak point with a large number of Incan soldiers, splitting

Naval Expedition

It was unusual for the Incas to fight on water. However, the late-fifteenth-century emperor Topa Inca Yupanqui launched a rare naval invasion against the island-dwelling Puná, whose home was off the coast of Ecuador. This account appeared in Fernando Montesinos's *Memorias Antiguas Historiales del Peru,* written in the mid–seventeenth century, sometime after Montesinos's return to Spain from Peru.

"Many balsas [rafts] and good pilots were made ready. The army, which consisted of twenty thousand persons, embarked. They arrived at the island. The islanders [the Puná] came forth to meet the Inga [Inca]. Battle was joined. [At first] victory favoured them [the Puná], on account of their skill as sailors, not on account of their strength as soldiers. The Inga ordered his general to show a firm front to the enemy, and one night he landed with part of his army on the island. He drew up his squadron by the shore of the sea . . . , and he ordered that the houses be set afire, and those who remained on land fled, while those at sea surrendered. . . .

This victory caused so much fear in all the land, on account of the fact that the people of Puná were reputed to be valiant men, that all the people round about surrendered and sent messengers to the Inga."

the opposing army in half. The fragmented foe was then surrounded and overcome.

Frequently, the enemy fell back to an easily defended position, such as the top of a hill or a fort. If possible, the Incas would set fire to scrub grass surrounding the enemy soldiers and burn them out. Otherwise, the Incan warriors would either storm the stronghold, overrunning the defenders, or set up a siege and wait for their foe to run out of food and water.

If the war dragged on, the Incas pushed hard at the enemy's resources. Of a campaign against the Chincha, a coastal people, the sixteenth-century author Garcilaso de la Vega wrote,

> The [Incan] general began to intensify the war against the Chinchas, investing [pressing] them more closely and laying waste their crops and the fruits of the field, so that they might be straitened by hunger. He had the irrigation canals destroyed, so that any land not laid waste by the Incas could not be watered. This had the greatest effect . . . [for] the country is so hot and the sun burns, the land has to be watered every three or four days. Or it will not bear fruit.[51]

Sixteenth-century Spanish author Garcilaso de la Vega chronicled in some detail many Incan battles.

Weapons

The weapons of the Incas were often superior to those of the enemy and played an important role in the crushing defeats frequently dealt Incan enemies. The Incan army was equipped with a variety of weapons. Customarily, troops who were similarly armed fought together. As the Incan force neared the enemy, warriors with slings hurled egg-sized stones with great force. At the same time, archers added arrows to the fray.

As the armies came closer, Incan soldiers brought down enemy warriors with bolas. The bola is a series of leather straps tied together with rocks at the ends of each strap. Bola throwers aimed for the legs. When the bola hit its target it wrapped itself around and around, pinning the legs together as effectively as if they were bound with ropes and bringing the victim crashing to the ground.

When the two sides finally closed in, Incan soldiers rushed forward swinging clubs and axes. A favorite club, the *macana*, had a multipointed stone or piece of metal fastened

Victory Procession

In his sixteenth-century *Narrative of the Incas,* Juan de Betanzos describes Emperor Pachacuti Inca Yupanqui's return to Cuzco after the conquest of the Soras, a people who lived about two hundred miles south of Cuzco.

"When they came within sight of the city of Cuzco, he [the emperor] ordered . . . [his] captains to assemble there all together with him and to enter the city singing . . . about the things that had happened on the expedition. . . . At the same time he ordered the prisoners [Soras leaders] to cry and declare their guilt and crimes in a loud voice and how they were subjects and vassals of the son of the Sun and that no forces could resist him. . . .

In this way the Inca entered Cuzco where, as he reached the square, he found there the statue of the Sun and the statues of . . . the ancient lords [royal mummies]. . . . On arriving, the Inca made his gestures of obeisance [bows] and sacrifices. Afterward, he ordered that . . . tigers [jaguars] be placed in a house that he had designated for a jail. . . . With these fierce animals in there, he ordered that the prisoners be thrown in there so that the tigers would eat them. And he ordered that the prisoners be kept in the company of these fierce animals for three days. If after three days the tigers had not eaten them, the survivors were to be let out. Since the tigers had not eaten for two days, they say that they ate I do not know how many of them. Those who were found alive after three days were taken out."

to its end. The heads of the battle-axes were stone or copper, silver, or gold, depending on the bearer's rank. Some warriors also threw small, dartlike javelins, while others thrust at enemy warriors with longer spears.

Armor and Helmets

For protection, each soldier carried on his arm a round or square shield. Made of wood, these shields were covered with either metal or deerskin, over which was stretched a cloth bearing a painted or woven design. A second shield made of cotton or palm slats hung down each warrior's back.

Protection in battle was also provided by quilted cotton suits and wooden or cotton helmets. Copper, silver, and gold disks worn front and back and indicating rank offered further protection. Finally, each warrior wore a long shawl that he could wrap around an arm and use as a shield.

Victory

When well-armed Incan warriors attacked their enemy, they did not seek to take prisoners. They sought to capture only important leaders during battle. The main objective was to kill as many of the enemy as possible to demoralize a foe. After the battle, Incan soldiers often made flutes out of the bones of the dead enemy. Surviving enemy warriors, however, were not mistreated. Along with thousands of women and children from the defeated land, the Incas marched their prisoners to Cuzco to be shown off in a triumphant victory parade. The defeated warriors were then made to lie on their bellies, while the emperor walked across their backs. Then, most of the captives

Rebellion

A year after Topa Inca Yupanqui became emperor in 1471 he was faced with a rebellion of an imperial province. The story of the rebellion is recounted in Juan de Betanzos's sixteenth-century *Narrative of the Incas*.

"Topa Inca Yupanqui was in the city of Cuzco . . . making arrangements . . . for the good government and the provision of the things needed in the city . . . [when an] *orejones* [noble] . . . arrived in the city. . . . He told . . . that the province of the Andes was in rebellion. . . . One night they [the rebels] surrounded all of those [Incan soldiers] who were on guard, and so many men surrounded them that not one man could escape except him. . . . In a short time all the guards were killed. And when they were dead, their flesh was handed out among the rebels. He [the noble] had escaped by submerging himself in a river. With his head covered by some trees and bushes he saw the rebels come to wash the flesh of the dead. In this way he had escaped coming up the river at night.

When Topa Inca Yupanqui learned the news about the rebellion . . . , he got very angry. He had honored them in conquering them and by doing it himself. He immediately ordered an assembly of his warriors . . . to go out and conquer . . . [the province of the Andes] again. . . . Topa Inca Yupanqui left Cuzco with his warriors very well equipped and prepared. . . . The Inca's soldiers chased them [the rebels] down, capturing and killing all the lords of the Andes who had rebelled against the Inca."

---

were released and allowed to return home. The empire wanted workers, not dead prisoners.

The emperor did order the execution or sacrifice of the most important enemy leaders. Many of these prisoners died in underground cells filled with hungry predators or venomous snakes. The seventeenth-century writer Bernabe Cobo tells the fate of rebel leaders during the reign of Topa Inca: "He [Topa Inca] had the two main caciques [chiefs] skinned and he ordered two drums to be made from their hides."[52]

The Spoils of War

The Sapa Inca gave unmarried captive women as gifts to his officers. To these aristocrats, the Incan ruler also handed out promotions and special privileges, such as the right to ride in a litter or sit on a stool.

Imperial gifts were also given to common soldiers. They were offered in exchange for service in a dangerous enterprise. According to the sixteenth-century Spanish chronicler Juan de Betanzos, the emperor Topa Inca "had all his soldiers assemble. . . . Wishing to pay them for the services they had rendered to him, . . . he did great favors for all of them, by giving them many women, valuables, and livestock, all of which had been taken as spoils from the enemy."[53]

Keys to Victory

The Incas did not always win their military campaigns. They had little success in conquering the rain-forest lands that lapped the eastern slopes of the Peruvian Andes or in fully subduing the people of central Chile or northern Ecuador. However, the Incas were usually victorious.

The Incas won the majority of their wars because their army was large and well equipped. Furthermore, their strategy and tactics, though simple, combined with competent leadership to make an effective fighting force.

Generally, after a major victory, the empire had little trouble with the subdued civilian population. Just the sight of such a large, well-armed army marching through the land was enough to intimidate those who did not bear arms.

Equally important to the success of the Incan army was that it could move efficiently to reach enemies and that it could keep itself easily supplied. These feats were possible because of the extensive road system that crisscrossed the Inca Empire. Incan engineering, however, served not only the military but the entire society.

CHAPTER 7

The Builders

The Incas were master builders. They created a huge network of roads that crisscrossed the empire and tied its farthest reaches to the capital at Cuzco. Working mostly with stone, the Incas constructed entire cities, filled with public buildings of monumental size. Furthermore, to give themselves more farmland in their mountainous homeland, they carved agricultural terraces out of the sides of mountains.

The engineers and architects who designed these projects were part of the Incan aristocracy and were extremely skilled at their jobs. Indeed, many of the monumental projects of the Incas have survived to the present. Civil engineer Kenneth R. Wright and archaeologist Alfredo Valencia Zegarra point out that "the well-preserved remains of [the Incan city of] Machu Picchu show that they had an advanced understanding of such principles as urban planning, . . . drainage, and durable construction methods."[54]

The Roads

Planning and constructing roads was one of the major tasks of the engineers. The actual building and upkeep of the roads was the task of common laborers as part of their *mit'a* duty. For a century beginning in the early 1400s, the Incan commoners laid down and repaired fourteen thousand miles of roads. Two main roads ran north and south. One was in the highlands and began in northern Ecuador, passed through Cuzco, and ended in Argentina. The second ran along the coast from the present-day Ecuador-Peru border and south into Chile. A network of roads branched from these trunk lines, connecting them and all the major cities of the empire, as well as leading to the imperial borders. The roads also ran to important shrines and holy sites.

Because the Incas did not have the wheel and thus no rolling vehicles, they built roads for foot travel and llama pack trains. The roads, therefore, were not always flat. Over level terrain, workers paved the roadbed with flat stones. They began by building a roadbed of earth piled high. They then built a wall on either side of the bed to hold it in place. These walls could be as high as twelve feet.

When the road reached mountains, the laborers often carved steps up the steep slopes. If the rock barrier they faced was not too thick, they would sometimes tunnel through the stone. The workers created tunnels by enlarging natural fissures, or cracks, in the rock.

The Incas did not have any standard road width or layout. Thus, in some places the roads were eighty feet wide, while in others they shrank to no more than a footpath. Sometimes, these routes went straight up and down slopes; in other places they curved gently around hills.

Standardized or not, the roads were impressive. They were also well maintained. Writing about one road section, the sixteenth-century Spanish soldier Pedro de Cieza de

León said, "In the time of the Lord-Incas it was clean, without a stone or blade of grass, for they were always looking after it."[55]

Bridges

To cross highland rivers—which were deep, fast flowing, and often at the bottom of canyons—the Incas built bridges. Workers slung ropes across a river and then anchored them to wooden towers on the banks. Between the ropes, the Incas suspended a wooden walkway. The regular replacement of the ropes kept a number of these bridges in operation well into the nineteenth century.

In the coastal lowlands, where riverbanks were lower and the water flowed more slowly, workers built stone and wooden bridges. Occasionally, they constructed pontoon bridges. The flooring of these bridges was made of wood and floated on huge pontoons, or bundles, made of dried reed.

Messengers

Imperial roads allowed for relatively speedy delivery of messages and news to any point in the empire. Threats of invasion or rebellion, for instance, reached Cuzco via messengers running these roads. The response was an army marching back along the same route. Strings of runners also carried orders or quipu from Cuzco to provincial capitals.

Messengers, known as *chaski*, were posted every ten to fifteen miles at way stations that lined the roads. At each station were small huts in which two runners lived. While one slept, the other awaited messages that he would carry to the next way station. Sixteenth-century Incan descendant Huamán Poma described the *chaski*:

> They were usually of good family and were famous for their loyalty. They wore a sunbonnet of white feathers so that they could be seen from a long way off by other messengers.... [They carried a shell] trumpet

Roadway

The Incan roads were the lifeline of the empire. Here, from *History of the Inca Empire*, the seventeenth-century Jesuit Bernabe Cobo, who lived most of his adult life in Peru, describes one of the roads that led up into the Andes.

"This road of ... the sierra [mountains] and broken land was made by hand with much work and skill. If it passed through hillsides with cliffs and slabs of rock, a narrow path, only wide enough for one person leading a llama ..., was dug in the boulder itself, and this type of construction did not run very far, but as soon as the boulder or slab of rock was passed, the road widened again. On some rugged slopes where the road could not be made across the middle of the hillside, strong steps were made of flat stones.... Across all the other ... slopes, the road was ... leveled off and ten or twelve feet wide. Where the slope was very steep, there was a wall of [stone] ... and inside it was filled up with earth so that it was made even and perfectly level ... ; in other places, on the upper side [of the slope], they had a wall made of stone without mortar ... that would hold back the earth and rocks that rolled down from above, so that the road would not be blocked.... Where there was some ravine or narrow gorge that cut off the road [if not too deep], walls were also made from below and built up to the level of the road."

The Builders

... [with which] to alert the next runner at the relay station by a blast of sound from the approaching chaski. They were armed with a cudgel [club] and a sling and were maintained at the Inca's expense, being authorized to draw food and other stores from his warehouses all over the country.[56]

In this fashion, messages traveled 125 to 150 miles a day. As an example, a royal order from Cuzco could reach Quito in Ecuador, some 800 miles away, in five or six days. Some 375 *chaski* were required to carry a message that distance.

Traveling the Roads

Walking on an Incan road required official permission. For the most part, roads were re-

Incan engineers carved staircases out of rock to help travelers make their way along the steep slopes of the Andes.

stricted to military personnel and those on state business. Imperial officials, either on inspection trips or being transferred to the provinces, were among these latter travelers.

Other travelers transported corn, coca, metal, textiles, feathers, and other goods for the state. This traffic was either headed to Cuzco for the use of the emperor and the Incan aristocracy or on its way as imperial gifts to important *curacas*.

The general population normally kept off the roads, except when as *mit'a* workers they were required to build or repair them. Thus, the roads remained clear and open to official traffic.

Rest Stops

Along the road were small settlements called *tambos*. Each *tambo* had a low-ceiling building in which travelers could spend the night. There was also a corral for llamas. A caretaker ensured that the *tambo* was kept fully stocked.

The emperor himself occasionally toured the empire, and his party would find shelter in the *tambos*. Likewise, the army would also stop at the road settlements, but they would pitch tents to accommodate their numbers.

Symbols of Authority

The roads were more than a communication and transportation system. They were also a symbol of Incan power. Archaeologist John Hyslop observes,

> To conquered populations throughout the Inka empire, the roads were an omnipresent [universal] symbol of the power and authority of the Inka state. There were probably very few individuals subject to the

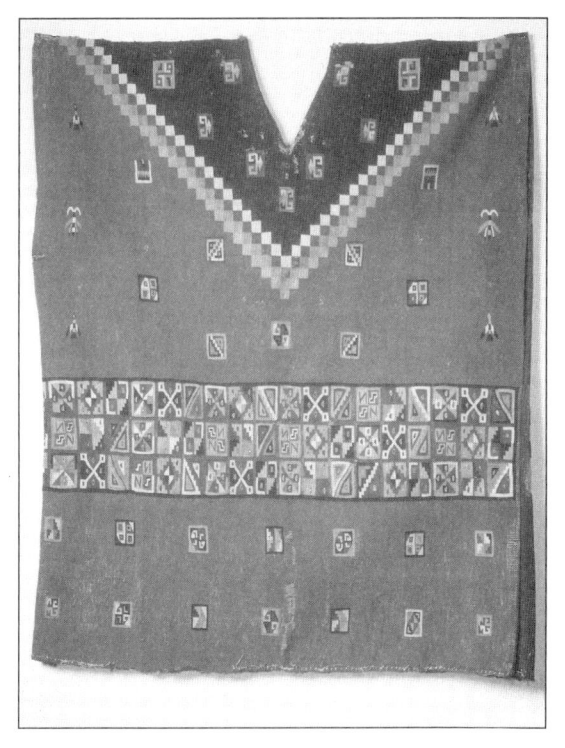

Traders who traveled Incan roads transported textiles and other important commodities.

Inka state who had never seen an Inka road, even though many of these individuals had . . . rarely seen an actual Inka from the region around Cuzco.[57]

Nor were the roads the only constructions that announced imperial might. Incan public architecture in general was monumental in scale and size. It was meant to impress, to awe, to overwhelm, leading archaeologists Graciano Gasparini and Luise Margolies to call it "architecture of power."[58]

In the Incan capital of Cuzco, for example, Coricancha, the main temple, had a perimeter of twelve hundred feet. On its exterior walls were plates of gold that caught and reflected sunlight. Atop a hill at the city's north end was another example of this architecture of power: the Sacsahuaman, a massive structure whose walls were made of stones measuring thirteen feet high. It could hold as many as five thousand people.

The purpose of the Sacsahuaman is something of a mystery. Its size and its high placement argue that it might have been a fortress. Another possible use was as a site for religious ceremonies. It also appears to have served as a storehouse since many of its rooms were filled with weapons, pottery, jewelry, and clothing.

The construction of the many roads and public buildings served the empire in another way as well. It kept imperial subjects hard at work. Some of the building projects used up to thirty thousand laborers at a time. Thus, between tending their fields and performing their labor for the state, commoners had little time for recreation, let alone plotting rebellion.

Tight Fit

Size was not the only impressive feature of imperial public buildings. The walls of these structures revealed the remarkable Incan stonework. The stones fit so tightly, one to another, that the Spanish discovered later that a knife blade could not slip between them.

Incan public buildings had other shared traits. They were almost always rectangular, and doors, windows, and wall niches were trapezoids. A trapezoid is a four-sided figure with only two parallel sides. Incan doors, for instance, were narrower at the top than at the bottom. These buildings were also generally only one story high. The Incas preferred to spread out horizontally rather than vertically.

In the Cuzco area and in provincial capitals, such public buildings were common. They were less so in other cities in the empire. Unless the imperial officials were constructing a city from scratch, they contented themselves with adding a few government buildings and temples to already existing urban centers. These new structures marked the city as Incan property.

Planning

Incan construction depended on measurements. Imperial units of length were based on parts of the human body and therefore were somewhat variable. The smallest unit was the distance between the outstretched thumb and forefinger, approximately 5 inches; the palm came next, 8 inches; the forearm, 18 inches; and the height of a man, 64 inches. The last was the only one of these units that was standardized. The Incas had sticks cut to that length with which they could make exact measurements. The Incas also had a standard unit of area, the *topo,* that was approximately 300 feet by 150 feet.

Construction also depended on having some sort of plan. Therefore, before beginning a construction project, Incan architects would build detailed models of the proposed work out of clay or stone.

The Site

When going from model to building, Incan engineers often found it necessary to reshape the land of the proposed site. They did not change the design of the building. Thus, if it was necessary, the Incas leveled hills, filled in depressions, and did whatever else was needed to make the site suitable for replicating the model.

In part, this practice of making the land fit the building came from a belief in Incan power over nature. But it also arose simply from a desire to build in specific places. Whenever possible, the Incas wanted their public buildings to look out over rivers, mountains, or lagoons.

Sites were also chosen to ensure that administrative centers could be easily reached and supplied.

Obtaining the Raw Material

As with all work, *mit'a* laborers supplied the muscle to erect a building. They broke each stone block (which could weigh as much as fourteen tons) free from quarry walls by pounding wooden wedges into cracks with stone hammers. This method was the same one used by Incan miners to drive tunnels through rock faces.

Then, the laborers moved the block to the construction site. The exact method they used is not known. Possibly, gangs of workmen jockeyed the massive object there using wooden poles. They would slip the ends of their poles under the block and rock it back and forth and finally forward. Progress would have been slow.

Construction

At the construction site, other workers dug trenches for the building's foundation. They laid down a layer of small stones and then, using increasingly bigger rock, built the foundation up to ground level.

The wall grew from ground level up a layer at a time. The laborers alternated placing rocks lengthwise and then crosswise, thus increasing the stability. To move the rocks into place, dirt

Incan Construction

By studying surviving Incan buildings, archaeologists have learned how the Incas erected the walls of these structures. In their book *Machu Picchu,* Kenneth R. Wright and Alfredo Valencia Zegarra describe the process that began with the Incas digging a trench deep into the ground.

"The Inca technique for constructing wall foundations started with the careful placement of smaller rocks in the excavation [trench] bottom to create a firm bedding. The rocks became larger as the foundation rose nearer the ground. A typical wall was . . . 2.6 feet thick at the groundline. . . . In some instances, the Incan engineers selected a . . . granite rock [that was part of the ground] . . . for their foundation . . . , which was first shaped to provide a ledge or platform for [the foundation]. Examples include the Temple of the Sun [in Machu Picchu]. . . .

In wall construction, the building stones were alternately placed in the wall lengthwise and then crosswise for stability. . . . Many of the stones have top and bottom indentations that helped fit them together in a nesting manner. Corner stones nearly always have such indentations to provide additional stability. . . . Mortar consisting of clay and earth mixed with small stones was used in many of the walls. . . .

At Machu Picchu at least 18 different stone wall types and patterns range from the finest carving and shaping to the roughest type of permanent construction for use in agricultural terraces. There are even examples of rough, temporary construction stone walls used as an inclined plane for moving large blocks upward."

The Builders

ramps were built against each wall. As the walls grew, so did the height of the ramps.

In actuality, each wall was two walls, one forming the exterior face of the building and the other the interior. In between was empty space. To tie the two parts of the wall together and to give added support, at intervals, *mit'a* laborers placed large rocks that spanned the gap and extended from one face to the other.

The workers then poured mortar—a mixture of clay, earth, and small stones—into the gap.

Smoothing the Edges

To achieve the finished look, Incan stonemasons, stone-working specialists, carefully chipped away at rocks dragged from quarries. They used

The massive stones of this Incan fortress were cut so flawlessly that their seams are extremely tight. How they were fit together so precisely remains a mystery.

The Rebuilding of Cuzco

In the mid–fifteenth century, the emperor Pachacuti Inca Yupanqui directed the transformation of Cuzco from a village of modest huts to a capital city of monumental stone buildings. The sixteenth-century Spanish writer Juan de Betanzos relates the story of the rebuilding in his *Narrative of the Incas*.

"Inca Yupanque [Yupanqui] and . . . the [Incan] lords . . . went around the outskirts of the city. . . . In this area they looked over the hills and places where they might find stone quarries and clay for making the mortar. . . . The Inca and the other lords . . . returned to the city. . . . Inca Yupanque outlined the city and had clay models made just as he planned to have it built. . . . [After he had ordered workers to be assembled, he ordered] some to transport rough stones for the foundation and others to bring the clay. . . . He ordered that all the springs be canalized [channeled] in such a way as to be piped to the houses of the city and to be made into fountains to supply water to the city. . . .

The Inca Yupanque ordered everyone from the city of Cuzco to leave their houses, take out everything they had in them, and go to the small towns nearby. . . . He ordered those houses to be torn down. . . . The Inca with his own hands . . . had a cord brought and measured with the cord the lot and houses that were to be made and their foundations and structures. With all of this prepared, the foundations were dug. . . . While these buildings were being made, the work went on continuously with fifty thousand Indians on the job. From the time that Inca Yupanque ordered the beginning of the improvements. . . , twenty years elapsed."

bronze chisels and stone hammers to shape the edges so that a rock nestled among its neighbors. From time to time, other workers lifted the stone into place so that the mason could check its fit. Then the *mit'a* laborers would heave the rock back out for the mason to continue his work. The last stage of creating a perfect fit required the mason to tediously rub the stone's edges for hours with sand and water.

Such effort was lavished only on the visible parts of each block. Anthropologist George Bankes notes, "Although no mortar was used on the exterior face of the wall, in the interior the stones were rarely perfectly fitted and the cracks were filled with mud."[59]

After the walls were completed, *mit'a* laborers applied a coat of plaster made from clay to the interior walls and sometimes to the exterior. To make the floor, they laid down layers of sand, gravel, and larger stones.

Not every part of the building was made of stone. Wood was used for the roof and for doorways. Not having nails, the workmen tied the wood together with fiber rope.

Other Buildings

Not all Incan buildings were so elaborate or so labor intensive. Indeed, private dwellings, except for those of the very wealthy, were modest in scope.

Each commoner *ayllu* built all the buildings, mostly homes, found in its community. *Ayllu* members collected stones from nearby fields, often the ones removed for plowing, and then set these stones in a clay-based mortar.

When the construction was finished, the builders plastered the rough exterior and interior walls with clay and then painted the outer walls.

Commoners also used adobe bricks in constructing their homes. Adobe was made by mixing mud with dry reeds or straw and then leaving it out in the sun to dry. Coastal area residents, with their dry, hot climate, were particularly fond of building homes from adobe brick.

Cuzco

Cuzco was the crown jewel of Incan urban planning and probably the largest imperial city, with a population of one hundred thousand. It incorporated all the elements that the Incas considered important for an urban center: solid building foundations, good drainage, and a reliable water supply. Drainage is particularly important because standing water can undercut a building's foundation and bring down the greatest of structures. Wright and Zegarra note that "it is the drainage system that suffers when the engineering standard of care is low. The Inca drainage . . . is one of the ways the Incas demonstrated that they built their cities for longevity [long life]."[60]

According to tradition, the emperor Pachacuti Inca Yupanqui had designed the Incan capital, even pacing off the building sites himself. The legend claims that Pachacuti had laid the city out in the shape of a puma, or mountain lion. The head was the Sacsahuaman and the tail, a narrow section of the city built between two rivers, the Huatanay and Tullumayo. To give the geography a more tail-like appearance, the Incas supposedly straightened out the beds of the rivers.

At Cuzco's center were two plazas that were divided from each other by a third river, the Saphy. The eastern plaza was the main city square and was floored with sand that had been transported from the beaches of the Pacific.

At the city's heart were the Coricancha, the Inca's palace, the homes of Incas-by-blood, and the workshop of the Chosen Women. Except for permanent household staff, no one else was allowed to live within Cuzco.

On the city's edge were the homes of the Incas-by-privilege. Surrounding the city's core were agricultural fields. Then came residential neighborhoods, which housed visiting *curacas* and foreign dignitaries as well as artisans and *mit'a* workers. Cuzco was a physical representation of the Incan social order.

Other Cities

The Incas used Cuzco as a model for other cities. Nonetheless, Incan engineers were not slaves to its plan. In Cuzco, for example, the central streets formed a grid; that is, the streets crossed each other at right angles. In the outer sections of the city, on the other hand, the streets radiated out like the spokes of a wheel. In other Incan cities, designers used one pattern or the other, not both. Furthermore, plazas were found in the heart of Cuzco, but they were placed to the side or at the end of other towns.

Machu Picchu

With Machu Picchu, Incan engineers built a very specialized and unique city. The city was located fifty miles northwest of Cuzco on the eastern side of the Andes at an altitude of eight thousand feet. Unlike Cuzco and other Incan cities, Machu Picchu lacked many features normally found in Incan settlements. Archaeologist Karen Wise writes that missing are

> storage silos . . . and administrative buildings as might be expected for a center of state administration. The city lacks the features of a seat of government or of a town of mainly economic or military importance. Although the agricultural products of the area surrounding Machu Picchu—coca and other crops—may have been important to

Archaeological evidence suggests that the magnificent city of Machu Picchu was designed to serve as a religious retreat for the emperor.

The Builders

The Sacsahuaman

The largest structure in Cuzco was the Sacsahuaman, which seems to have functioned as a fortress, temple, and huge storehouse. The earliest description of the Sacsahuaman was by Francisco Pizarro's secretary Pedro Sancho in his 1534 work *An Account of the Conquest of Peru*.

"There is a very beautiful fortress of earth and stone with big windows that look over the city. . . . In it there are many chambers and a main round tower in the center made with four or five stories. . . . The stones of which it is made are very well worked and so well placed next to each other that it seems they do not have mortar, and the stones are so smooth. . . . There are so many habitations [rooms] and the tower that one person cannot see it all in one day. . . . It cannot be attacked or undermined [dug under] because it is located on an outcrop [of rock]. On the side facing the city, there is . . . one wall on a rugged mountain slope. On the other side, . . . there are three, [one behind the other and] one higher than the other. . . . They are of such big stones that no one who sees them would say that they have been placed there by the hand of man. . . . From wall to wall there is so much earth [filling the space] that three carts together can pass on top. . . . This entire fortress was a great storehouse of arms, clubs, lances, bows, arrows, axes, shields, heavy jackets of quilted cotton, and other weapons of different types. . . . There was cloth and much tin and lead with other metals, and much silver and some gold."

---

the empire, the city itself did not function . . . as an agricultural . . . center. Rather it was probably a retreat, . . . where the emperor went to engage in religious or other activities away from his capital city.[61]

What Inca engineers did provide the city with were many points from which the sun could be observed. Also, they laid out the city so that it had an excellent view of three nearby holy mountains. Machu Picchu thus appears to have been a religious retreat for the emperor.

Waterworks

Incan engineers also worked on more than just roads and buildings. To water farmland, the engineers constructed irrigation systems. Teams of workers dug canals, some two feet wide and miles long, to bring water from rivers to croplands. These canals were sometimes lined with stone and covered to keep water from seeping into the ground or evaporating away. The engineers also had their *mit'a* laborers build stone aqueducts across gullies. Finally, they built reservoirs to hold water for times of drought.

Agricultural Terraces

Since much of the land in the Andes is mountainous, level ground is at a premium. The Incas constructed their own level ground. They built stone walls at intervals up and down the steep sides of mountains near their cities and towns. Then, they filled in the area behind the walls with rubble and then with one and a half feet of rich topsoil. The walls slanted slightly inward to better hold the soil. Such construction projects created terraces of level farmland that climbed like stairs up the mountainside.

These agricultural terraces vastly increased available cropland. The upper terraces, where the slope was steepest, were fairly narrow, about five feet wide. However, the lower ones were several acres in size.

Water for the terraces came from two sources. An irrigation canal fed water to the fields. In addition, stone staircases, which allowed farmers to move from terrace to terrace, served as channels that fed water from any mountain lakes or pools found in the upper reaches of the mountain.

The terraces benefited the Incas in ways other than farming. First, they reduced the risk of erosion and landslide by stabilizing the slopes on which they were built. Second, they were another form of architecture of power, as they demonstrated to imperial subjects the Incas' power over the rugged landscape.

The accomplishments of the Incas as builders did indeed awe their subjects. They even stunned the Spanish. But in the end, Incan architecture of power did not stop the European invaders from attacking and conquering the Inca Empire.

Epilogue: The End of Empire

At the beginning of the sixteenth century, the Inca Empire appeared strong and vigorous, its people and its enemies seemingly under control. Its roads and public buildings were a constant reminder of the Incas' might and power. Yet that might and power was about to be challenged by a foe unlike any this Andean people had ever known, the Spanish conquistadors.

Even before the Spanish arrived in 1532, the empire was having its troubles. Indeed, the last decade of imperial rule was a stormy period, marked by disease and civil war. And then came the Spanish invasion. Under these hammer blows of misfortune, the empire crumpled. Its collapse was hastened by its subject peoples' grasping the opportunity to break free of Incan control. In the end, Incas and non-Incas alike found themselves under new rulers, the Spanish.

Old and New Ways

The Incas, however, did not disappear, nor did their way of life. The Spanish found it useful to adopt many of the practices of the old empire. For instance, they found the *ayllu* system a useful way to monitor and control their new lands. They even allowed some of the old aristocracy to retain their power, just as the Incas themselves had allowed subject people to keep their old leaders.

In only one respect did the Spanish actively and fiercely work to change Incan ways. That was religion. To the European conquerors, the Incan religion was a form of devil worship, and it, along with all its temples and relics, had to be destroyed.

The Old Religion and the New

This effort by the Spanish was only partially successful. They pulled down the temples, even building a church over the main temple in Cuzco. They burned the royal mummies and many other sacred relics. And the old Incan religion disappeared, at least as it was practiced under the Sapa Inca.

However, many of the features of the old religion were folded into Spanish Catholicism. For instance, Christmas and the Incan festival Capac Raymi fall around the same time, and over time, such elements of the Incan ritual as dancing, singing, and drinking *chicha* merged with the Christian celebration.

After the Spanish conquest, *huacas* still existed in the Andes. Various sites, particularly mountains, continued to be the dwelling places of spirits. Many Andeans saw the major Catholic festival Corpus Christi as a chance to visit mountain *huacas* and make offerings of *chicha*. In addition, the idea that the earth was still ruled by Pacha-Mama was common among the descendants of the Incas, perhaps because their homeland was still racked by earthquakes and threatened by volcanoes.

Land and Family

Other aspects of the Incan way of life remained strong. In western South America, it was the old home of the Incas, the Andes highlands, where those aspects were most clearly seen. In the mountains, in addition to Spanish, people still spoke Quechua, which could be heard in markets and streets throughout the region. Many Andeans preferred the Incan language, rather than Spanish, in describing their relationships to other family members.

Despite the introduction of Western crops and animals, many farmers in the Andes stayed with the old Incan standards: corn, beans, squash, and potatoes. They still ate guinea pigs

Many Andean people live just as their Incan ancestors did. They speak the Quechua language, wear handwoven multicolored clothing, and farm using traditional implements.

The End of Empire

and raised alpacas and llamas for their wool. In the more distant parts of the Andes, people still used the llama as a pack animal. Mules and horses might carry larger loads, but llamas were more surefooted.

Farming in the highlands was still done on fields that the Incas had built. Also, as in Incan times, the produce of many farms was mostly for the use of the farmers and their families rather than being sold in town markets.

Furthermore, *ayllus* continued to control land, both cropland and pasture, parceling it out to each household, just as they had in Incan times. And, as their ancestors did, all the members of an Andean *ayllu* worked to maintain the group's irrigation canals.

According to historian Rebecca Stone-Miller, much of the Incan way of life remains intact even in modern times: "Despite the profound changes of the last 500 years, the Andean people have maintained a . . . vital continuity with their . . . past."[62] In the end, the Incas' way of life proved durable and vital. That way of life is the legacy of the Incas. As archaeologist Michael A. Malpass puts it:

> Perhaps the most enduring legacy of the Incas is the extent of change they brought to the groups they conquered. It was the Incas' goal to . . . level the dramatic political and social differences that had existed between groups prior to the Inca expansion. To do this, they moved individuals and entire villages around the empire, breaking up larger societies and lumping smaller ones into administrative units of equal size. They introduced the Quechua language to their subjects, and it persists to this day. . . . The sense of common culture that millions of Andean people share today is more the result of the Incas' policies than those of the Spaniards. . . . Thus it is difficult to say that the Incas no longer exist; . . . Inca culture is very much alive today—although in a modified form. This heritage is the greatest tribute to the Incas' impact on western South America.[63]

Notes

Introduction: A High-Altitude Civilization

1. Michael E. Moseley, *The Incas and Their Ancestors: The Archaeology of Peru*. London: Thames and Hudson, 1992, p. 7.
2. Pedro de Cieza de León, *The Incas*, ed. Victor Wolfgang von Hagen, trans. Harriet de Onis. Norman: University of Oklahoma Press, 1959, pp. 18–19.
3. Brian M. Fagan, *Kingdoms of Gold, Kingdoms of Jade: The Americas Before Columbus*. London: Thames and Hudson, 1991, p. 41.

Chapter 1: An Ordered World

4. Quoted in Edward Hyams and George Ordish, *The Last of the Incas*. London: Longmans, 1963, p. 37.
5. Quoted in Terence N. D'Altroy, *The Incas*. Malden, MA: Blackwell, 2002, pp. 94–95.
6. Ann Kendall, *Everyday Life of the Incas*. London: B.T. Batsford, 1973, p. 65.
7. Nigel Davies, *The Incas*. Niwot: University Press of Colorado, 1995, p. 114.
8. Fernando Montesinos, *Memorias Antiguas Historiales del Peru (Report of the Ancient History of Peru)*, ed. and trans. Philip Ainsworth Means. Nendeln, Liechtenstein: Kraus, 1920, p. 81.
9. Moseley, *The Incas and Their Ancestors*, p. 53.
10. María Rostworowski de Diez Canseco, *History of the Inca Realm*, trans. Harry B. Iceland. Cambridge, England: Cambridge University Press, 1999, pp. 15–16.
11. Cieza de León, *The Incas*, p. 221.

Chapter 2: Bureaucrats and Taxpayers

12. Quoted in Laura Laurencich Minelli, ed., *The Inca World: The Development of Pre-Columbian Peru, A.D. 1000–1534*. Norman: University of Oklahoma Press, 1999, p. 180.
13. Louis Baudin, *Daily Life in Peru Under the Last Incas*, trans. Winifred Bradford. New York: Macmillan, 1961, p. 223.
14. Quoted in Craig Morris and Donald E. Thompson, *Huánuco Pampa: An Inca City and Its Hinterlands*. London: Thames and Hudson, 1985, pp. 99–100.
15. Morris and Thompson, *Huánuco Pampa*, pp. 93–94.
16. Quoted in Clements R. Markham, ed. and trans., *Narratives of the Rites and Laws of the Yncas*. New York: Burt Franklin, 1873, p. 157.
17. Craig Morris and Adriana von Hagen, *The Inka Empire and Its Andean Origins*. New York: Abbeville Press, 1993, p. 114.
18. Huamán Poma, *Letter to a King: A Picture-History of the Inca Civilization*, ed. Christopher Dilke, trans. Nueva Corónica y Buen Gobierno. London: Allen & Unwin, 1978, p. 98.
19. Rebecca Stone-Miller, *Art of the Andes: From Chavín to Inca*. London: Thames and Hudson, 2002, p. 185.
20. Quoted in Markham, *Narratives of the Rites and Laws of the Yncas*, p. 155.

Chapter 3: Private Life

21. Garcilaso de la Vega, *Royal Commentaries of the Incas and General History of Peru*, trans. Harold V. Livermore, vol. 1. Austin: University of Texas Press, 1966 p. 212.
22. Quoted in Kendall, *Everyday Life of the Incas*, p. 77.
23. Quoted in Julian H. Steward, ed., *Handbook of South American Indians*, vol. 2,

The Andean Civilizations. Washington, DC: Smithsonian, 1946, p. 282.
24. Michael A. Malpass, *Daily Life in the Inca Empire.* Westport, CT: Greenwood Press, 1996, p. 78.
25. Quoted in Kendall, *Everyday Life of the Incas*, p. 128.
26. Malpass, *Daily Life in the Inca Empire*, pp. 79–80.
27. Juan de Betanzos, *Narrative of the Incas*, ed. and trans. Roland Hamilton and Dana Buchanan. Austin: University of Texas Press, 1996, p. 67.

Chapter 4: Priests and Worshippers

28. Baudin, *Daily Life in Peru Under the Last Incas*, p. 67.
29. Constance Classen, *Inca Cosmology and the Human Body.* Salt Lake City: University of Utah Press, 1993, p. 125.
30. Fagan, *Kingdoms of Gold, Kingdoms of Jade*, p. 48.
31. Quoted in Classen, *Inca Cosmology and the Human Body*, pp. 65–66.
32. Kendall, *Everyday Life of the Incas*, p. 192.
33. George Bankes, *Peru Before Pizarro.* Oxford, England: Phaidon Press, 1977, p. 117.
34. Bankes, *Peru Before Pizarro*, pp. 153–54.
35. Quoted in Markham, *Narratives of the Rites and Laws of the Yncas*, p. 13.
36. Quoted in George A. Collier, Renato I. Rosaldo, and John D. Wirth, eds., *The Inca and Aztec States, 1400–1800: Anthropology and History.* New York: Academic Press, 1982, pp. 109–10.
37. Quoted in Classen, *Inca Cosmology and the Human Body*, p. 64.

Chapter 5: Working Life

38. Moseley, *The Incas and Their Ancestors*, p. 43.

39. D'Altroy, *The Incas*, p. 276.
40. Edward P. Lanning, *Peru Before the Incas.* Englewood Cliffs, NJ: Prentice-Hall, 1967, p. 161.
41. Kendall, *Everyday Life of the Incas*, p. 152.
42. Quoted in Markham, *Narratives of the Rites and Laws of the Yncas*, p. 10.
43. Quoted in Markham, *Narratives of the Rites and Laws of the Yncas*, p. 168.
44. Malpass, *Daily Life in the Inca Empire*, p. 87.
45. Garcilaso, *Royal Commentaries of the Incas*, vol. 1, pp. 126–27.

Chapter 6: Army Life

46. Davies, *The Incas*, p. 148.
47. Baudin, *Daily Life in Peru Under the Last Incas*, pp. 132–33.
48. Rostworowski, *History of the Inca Realm*, p. 93.
49. John Hyslop, *Inka Settlement Planning.* Austin: University of Texas Press, 1990, p. 148.
50. Quoted in Terence N. D'Altroy, *Provincial Power in the Inka Empire.* Washington, DC: Smithsonian Institution Press, 1992, p. 78.
51. Garcilaso, *Royal Commentaries of the Incas*, vol. 1, p. 352.
52. Bernabe Cobo, *History of the Inca Empire*, ed. and trans. Roland Hamilton. Austin: University of Texas Press, 1979, p. 143.
53. Betanzos, *Narrative of the Incas*, p. 147.

Chapter 7: The Builders

54. Kenneth R. Wright and Alfredo Valencia Zegarra, *Machu Picchu: A Civil Engineering Marvel.* Reston, VA: American Society of Civil Engineers, 2000, p. 1.
55. Cieza León, *The Incas*, p. 136.

56. Poma, *Letter to a King*, p. 99.
57. John Hyslop, *The Inka Road System*. Orlando, FL: Academic Press, 1984, p. 2.
58. Quoted in Morris and Thompson, *Huánuco Pampa*, p. 89.
59. Bankes, *Peru Before Pizarro*, p. 193.
60. Wright and Zegarra, *Machu Picchu*, p. 36.
61. Quoted in Paul G. Bahn, ed., *Lost Cities*. New York: Welcome Rain, 1997, p. 197.

Epilogue: The End of Empire

62. Stone-Miller, *Art of the Andes*, p. 218.
63. Malpass, *Daily Life in the Inca Empire*, pp. xxviii–xxix.

For Further Reading

Books

Michael Coe, Dean Snow, and Elizabeth Benson, *Atlas of Ancient America.* New York: Facts On File, 1986. Filled with illustrations and maps, this reference work has a section on Incan culture that is packed with valuable information.

James A. Corrick, *The Inca.* San Diego: Lucent Books, 2001. This book relies on archaeological evidence and historical records to tell the story of the Incas, their wars, their conquests, their intrigues, and their accomplishments.

Daniele Kuss, *Incas.* New York: Marshall Cavendish, 1991. Filled with color illustrations, this retelling of Incan myths and legends also includes a useful discussion of the imperial religion.

Peter Lourie, *Lost Treasure of the Inca.* Honesdale, PA: Boyds Mills Press, 1999. The author describes his search for the lost treasure of the Incas. Color photographs of Incan gold jewelry and figures and a historical narrative link the present to the past.

Fiona MacDonald, *Inca Town.* New York: Franklin Watts, 1999. This book skillfully uses color drawings and cutaways to give the reader a view into Incan temples, homes, and workshops.

Elizabeth Mann, *Machu Picchu: The Story of the Amazing Inkas and Their City in the Clouds.* New York: Mikaya Press, 2000. This history of Machu Picchu details the Incas' building and use of the city. Full-page color illustrations, photographs, and maps supplement the text.

Hazel Mary Martell, *Civilizations of Peru Before 1535.* Austin, TX: Raintree Steck-Vaughn, 1999. Illustrations and maps help tell the stories of several ancient Peruvian civilizations, including the Incas, and the impact of the Spanish Conquest on these people.

Marion Morrison, *An Inca Farmer.* Vero Beach, FL: Rourke Enterprises, 1988. This unique book describes the life of an Incan farmer during the height of the empire.

Dennis Nishi, *The Inca Empire.* San Diego: Lucent Books, 2000. Filled with instructive illustrations, this work traces the rise and fall of the Inca Empire. It contains excerpts from period documents, maps, a time-line, and a reading list.

Matti A. Pitkanen, *The Grandchildren of the Incas.* Minneapolis, MN: Carolrhoda Books, 1991. This volume contrasts and compares the life of the present-day Quechua Indians of Peru with their Incan ancestors. Color photographs of the modern people capture the reality of their lives and homeland.

Johan Reinhard, *Discovering the Inca Ice Maiden: My Adventures on Ampato.* Washington, DC: National Geographic Society, 1998. This firsthand report tells of the 1995 discovery and study of the mummy of a young Incan girl found on the Peruvian volcano Mount Ampato. Along with the text are color photographs of the mummy and its artifacts.

Timothy R. Roberts, *Gods of the Maya, Aztecs, and Incas.* New York: MetroBooks, 1996. The author examines the beliefs and religious practices of the Incas, showing the effect of religion on everyday life and moral codes.

Tim Wood, *The Incas.* New York: Viking, 1996. Using double-page, peel-away transparencies, this work allows readers to look inside an Inca house, a temple, a palace, and a roadside way station.

Web Sites

The Incas: A Pictorial Tribute to Their Art and Culture (www.theincas.com). This site contains excellent color images of Incan stonework, pottery, and gold jewelry.

TeacherNet (http://members.aol.com/TeacherNet/Incas.html). This helpful site provides links to Incan history, language, culture, artifacts, and ruins.

Teacher Oz's Kingdom of History (www.teacheroz.com). This site has useful links to maps of the Inca Empire, Incan history and achievements, an account of the Spanish Conquest, Incan descendants, and details about Machu Picchu. (Click on home page's "Table of Contents" and then scroll down to the "Meso and Latin American" link.)

Works Consulted

Paul G. Bahn, ed., *Lost Cities*. New York: Welcome Rain, 1997. This collection of illustrated articles, written by archaeologists, describes some fifty ancient cities, including the Incan Machu Picchu.

George Bankes, *Peru Before Pizarro*. Oxford, England: Phaidon Press, 1977. This work looks at the social structures, governments, religious practices, and crafts of the Incas and their predecessors.

Louis Baudin, *Daily Life in Peru Under the Last Incas*. Trans. Winifred Bradford. New York: Macmillan, 1961. A noted Incan scholar paints a vivid picture of the public and private lives of the Incan nobility, bureaucrats, soldiers, priests, farmers, and artisans.

Juan de Betanzos, *Narrative of the Incas*. Ed. and trans. Roland Hamilton and Dana Buchanan. Austin: University of Texas Press, 1996. This sixteenth-century chronicle discusses the Inca Empire and the Spanish Conquest. The author, fluent in Quechua, the Inca language, interviewed many Incas, including those related to the old ruling family.

John Bierhorst, ed. and trans., *Black Rainbow: Legends of the Incas and Myths of Ancient Peru*. New York: Farrar, Straus, and Giroux, 1976. This collection presents Incan legends and myths that were originally collected by various Spanish writers.

Pedro de Cieza de León, *The Incas*. Ed. Victor Wolfgang von Hagen. Trans. Harriet de Onis. Norman: University of Oklahoma Press, 1959. This exhaustive chronicle of the Inca Empire is judged by historians as one of the best and most reliable of the sixteenth-century accounts. Its author was a soldier who served in Peru for several years, beginning in 1547.

Constance Classen, *Inca Cosmology and the Human Body*. Salt Lake City: University of Utah Press, 1993. This study describes Incan religious beliefs and practices, explaining how they affected Incan society.

Bernabe Cobo, *History of the Inca Empire*. Ed. and trans. Roland Hamilton. Austin: University of Texas Press, 1979. This volume contains selections from a classic seventeenth-century history of the Inca Empire, written by a Spanish Jesuit who spent most of his adult life in Peru.

George A. Collier, Renato I. Rosaldo, and John D. Wirth, eds., *The Inca and Aztec States, 1400–1800: Anthropology and History*. New York: Academic Press, 1982. This collection includes a number of scholarly essays discussing how the Incas administered their empire.

Terence N. D'Altroy, *The Incas*. Malden, MA: Blackwell, 2002. Using the most current research findings, a noted Incan scholar details the history and culture of the Incas.

———, *Provincial Power in the Inka Empire*. Washington, DC: Smithsonian Institution Press, 1992. Based on the author's own fieldwork, this study examines Incan political and military strategies used to control imperial provinces.

Nigel Davies, *The Incas*. Niwot: University Press of Colorado, 1995. A working archaeologist presents a good overview of the rise and fall of the Inca Empire.

Brian M. Fagan, *Kingdoms of Gold, Kingdoms of Jade: The Americas Before Columbus*. London: Thames and Hudson, 1991. In a concise, fact-filled chapter, a distinguished anthropologist covers the Inca Empire, along with other cultures of the Americas.

Garcilaso de la Vega, *The Incas: The Royal Commentaries of Garcilaso de la Vega 1539–1616.* Trans. Alan Gheerbrant. New York: Orion, 1961. This thorough sixteenth-century study is an important early history of the Inca Empire. The author was part Inca; his mother was a cousin of the last Incan ruler.

———, *Royal Commentaries of the Incas and General History of Peru.* Trans. Harold V. Livermore. 2 vols. Austin: University of Texas Press, 1966. This is a second English translation of Garcilaso's important work.

Edward Hyams and George Ordish, *The Last of the Incas.* London: Longmans, 1963. This volume offers a probing look at the final years of the Inca Empire and the internal conflicts and problems that led up to its conquest by the Spanish.

John Hyslop, *The Inka Road System.* Orlando, FL: Academic Press, 1984. An eminent archaeologist discusses in detail Incan roads, where they ran, how many there were, how many miles they covered, and how they were built.

———, *Inka Settlement Planning.* Austin: University of Texas Press, 1990. This book is a comprehensive survey of Incan urban planning as revealed through archaeological studies of a number of Incan cities.

Ann Kendall, *Everyday Life of the Incas.* London: B.T. Batsford, 1973. This study by a distinguished scholar discusses all aspects of Incan society, from public to private, as well as showing what life was like in the capital and in the provinces.

Edward P. Lanning, *Peru Before the Incas.* Englewood Cliffs, NJ: Prentice-Hall, 1967. This work presents the history and customs of ancient Peruvian cultures that, despite its title, includes the Incas.

Michael A. Malpass, *Daily Life in the Inca Empire.* Westport, CT: Greenwood Press, 1996. This prominent archaeologist first traces the history of the Incas and then discusses many aspects of Incan society, such as politics, private life, and religion.

Clements R. Markham, ed. and trans., *Narratives of the Rites and Laws of the Yncas.* New York: Burt Franklin, 1873. Dating from the sixteenth and seventeenth centuries, these four Spanish colonial documents describe Incan laws, customs, religion, and history. One is written by a native Andean.

Laura Laurencich Minelli, ed., *The Inca World: The Development of Pre-Columbian Peru, A.D. 1000–1534.* Norman: University of Oklahoma Press, 1999. Nicely illustrated with maps and color plates, this collection of essays by various scholars traces the rise and fall of Incan culture.

Fernando Montesinos, *Memorias Antiguas Historiales del Peru (Report of the Ancient History of Peru).* Ed. and trans. Philip Ainsworth Means. Nendeln, Liechtenstein: Kraus, 1920. The author, a seventeenth-century Jesuit who spent several years in Peru, provides worthwhile information about Incan cultures, despite a number of inaccuracies.

Craig Morris and Donald E. Thompson, *Huánuco Pampa: An Inca City and Its Hinterlands.* London: Thames and Hudson, 1985. This informative study details life in an Incan provincial town as uncovered by two archaeologists who excavated there.

Craig Morris and Adriana von Hagen, *The Inka Empire and Its Andean Origins.* New York: Abbeville Press, 1993. Color photographs enhance this clearly written study of the history and customs of the Incas.

Michael E. Moseley, *The Incas and Their Ancestors: The Archaeology of Peru.* London: Thames and Hudson, 1992. A prominent scholar's history of the Incas and other Andean cultures.

Huamán Poma, *Letter to a King: A Picture-History of the Inca Civilization.* Ed. Christopher Dilke. Trans. Nueva Corónica y Buen Gobierno. London: Allen & Unwin, 1978. Written in the late sixteenth century and illustrated by its author (a descendant of a high-ranking Incan official), this work offers a wealth of details about Incan culture.

María Rostworowski de Diez Canseco, *History of the Inca Realm.* Trans. Harry B. Iceland. Cambridge, England: Cambridge University Press, 1999. A celebrated Incan historian makes extensive use of original manuscripts of Spanish chronicles and colonial records to present the history of the Incas and detail the workings of their society.

Pedro Sancho, *An Account of the Conquest of Peru.* Trans. Philip Ainsworth Means. Boston: Milford House, 1917. The author, who took part in the conquest of the Incas, describes many aspects of Incan life.

Julian H. Steward, ed., *Handbook of South American Indians.* Vol. 2, *The Andean Civilizations.* Washington, DC: Smithsonian, 1946. This classic anthropological study of the Andean peoples has a long chapter describing the Incas.

Rebecca Stone-Miller, *Art of the Andes: From Chavín to Inca.* London: Thames and Hudson, 2002. This volume is an art historian's well-illustrated examination of the arts and crafts of several Andean cultures, ending with the Incas.

Kenneth R. Wright and Alfredo Valencia Zegarra, *Machu Picchu: A Civil Engineering Marvel.* Reston, VA: American Society of Civil Engineers, 2000. An experienced civil engineer and an eminent Peruvian archaeologist describe the construction of Machu Picchu in this thorough, well-illustrated study.

Index

accounting system, 65–66
Account of the Conquest of Peru, An (Sancho), 65, 90
administration, 22, 28–30
afterlife, 49
agricultural terraces, 90–91
　see also farming
alpacas, 25, 63
ancestry, 18
Andes mountains, 10
animal sacrifice, 54–55
apparel, 44–45
architecture, 10–11, 13, 24–25, 40, 49–51, 71–72, 83–84
aristocracy
　education of, 37
　marriage customs of, 38
　palaces of, 40
　privileges of, 16–17
　recreation of, 44, 45
　religion and, 49
　women of, 42–43
　work of, 28, 29
army
　battle plans of, 75
　clothing of, 72–73, 77
　feeding of, 17
　marching and, 72–74
　organization of, 70
　prisoner treatment by, 77–78
　protection for, 77
　tactics of, 75, 77–78
　training of, 70–71
　victories of, 77–79
　weapons of, 76–77
artists, 67
assets. See storehouses

babies, 34
Bankes, George, 52, 54, 87
barter system, 22, 25
bathing, 41
Baudin, Louis, 23, 46, 54
Betanzos, Juan de, 77, 78, 87
Bierhorst, John, 16
Black Rainbow (Bierhorst), 16
bridges, 81
buildings, 24–25, 40, 49–51, 53, 71–72, 84–88
bureaucracy, 22, 28–30

calendar, 57
Canseco, María Rostworowski de Diez. See Rostworowski de Diez de Canseco, María
capital. See Cuzco

Catholicism, 92
ceremonies
　coming-of-age, 37–39
　death, 58–59
　harvest, 56
　naming, 34, 37
　prayers for, 54
　preparation for, 57
　puberty, 37–39
　rituals of, 57–58
　sacrifice and, 54–56
　types of, 56–57
　war, 72
　wedding, 39–40
childhood, 34–38, 55–56
Chosen Women, 52–54, 57
churches. *See* religion; temples
Cieza de León, Pedro de. *See* León, Pedro de Cieza de
cities, 11, 88
　see also Cuzco; Machu Picchu
Classen, Constance, 47, 48
class structure, 15–17
　see also aristocracy; common people
climate, 60
cloth, 42, 45
clothing, 44–45
Cobo, Bernabe, 18, 78, 81
coca, 25
common people
　housing of, 40
　human sacrifice and, 55–56
　labor of, 84

marriage customs of, 38
origins of, 17
rebellion and, 84
recreation of, 45
religion and, 49
resettlement of, 32
restrictions on, 17
work of, 27–28, 60–63
see also servants
communication, 81–82
conquistadors, 11, 92–94
construction, 24–25, 40, 84–88
cooking, 43
counting, 65–66
crafts, 66–68
creation story, 46–48
crime and punishment, 30–32
crops, 60
　see also farming; food
Cuzco
　architecture of, 83–84
　description of, 88
　founding of, 10
　importance of, 13, 16, 20
　rebuilding of, 87

Daily Life in Peru Under the Last Incas (Baudin), 54
D'Altroy, Terence N., 20, 61, 68
dancing, 34
Davies, Nigel, 16, 70

death, 49, 58–59
defense. *See* army; fortresses
Diez Canseco, María Rostworowski de. *See* Rostworowski de Diez de Canseco, María
dining, 43–44
divorce, 17–18

eating, 43–44
education, 36–37
elite. *See* aristocracy
emperor
   appearance of, 14–15, 18
   death ritual for, 59
   power of, 14–15, 18, 21
   recreation of, 44
   religion and, 48, 50
   succession to position of, 21
engineering, 80–81, 84–85, 88–90
espionage, 75

fabric, 42, 45
Fagan, Brian M., 13, 47–48
fairs, 25, 45
family, 17–20, 29–30
farming, 27–28, 60–63
feathers, 45
festivals. *See* ceremonies; fairs
fishing, 63–64

food, 43–44, 52, 60, 62
fortresses, 71–72, 90
Four Quarters, land of, 11, 13

gambling, 45
Gamboa, Sarmiento de, 48
Garcilaso de la Vega
   on agriculture, 62
   on child raising, 34–35
   on education and knowledge, 36
   on manhood rites, 38
   on warfare, 76
   on weaving, 42
Gasparino, Graciano, 83
gods, 46–48
   see also religion
government, 13, 22, 28–30
   see also class structure; taxes
guinea pigs, 62

healers, 69
herding, 25
highways, 13, 80–83
History of the Inca Empire (Cobo), 18, 81
households, 17–20, 29–30
housekeeping, 42
housing, 40
Huánuco Pampa: An Inca City and Its Hinterlands (Morris and Thompson), 24, 25

human sacrifice, 55–57
hunting, 63
Hyslop, John, 71, 72, 83

Inca Cosmology and the Human Body (Classen), 48
Inca Empire
   archaeological research about, 13
   building of, 10–11, 13
   child-raising practices in, 34–37
   conquest of, 92–94
   culture of, 13
   customs of, 32
   economy of, 22–27
   end of, 92–94
   founder of, 14, 16, 38, 49
   harshness of life in, 34–35
   health care in, 69
   importance of, 10, 13
   languages of, 16, 32
   literature of, 68–69
   mountainous nature of, 10
   music of, 68–69
   names for, 11, 13
   nations emerging from, 10
   rulers of, 11
   territory covered by, 10, 12
   tolerance in, 32
   transportation in, 66
Incas: The Royal Commentaries, The (Garcilaso), 36, 38, 42, 57

Incas, The (D'Altroy), 20, 68
infancy, 34
Inka Settlement Planning (Hyslop), 71
irrigation, 90–91
   see also climate; farming

judicial system, 30–32

Kendall, Ann, 15, 52, 62
knots, 65–66

labor tax, 26–28
land management, 22–23
Land of the Four Quarters, 11, 13
Lanning, Edward P., 62
leaders, 11, 13, 39, 45, 47
   see also administration; aristocracy; emperor
legal system, 30–32
León, Pedro de Cieza de
   on corn harvest celebration, 57
   on imperial succession, 21
   on military campaigns, 74
   on road maintenance, 80–81
   on temple, 51
   on valleys, 10

Letter to a King: A Picture-History of the Inca Civilization (Poma), 29, 44
litter bearing, 66, 73
　see also roads; transportation
livestock, 25
llamas, 25, 54–55, 62–63
location, 10
luxury items, 14–15, 25

Machu Picchu, 85, 88–90
Machu Picchu: A Civil Engineering Marvel, (Wright and Zegarra), 85
Malpass, Michael A., 37, 42–43, 68, 94
Manco Capac, 14, 16, 38, 49
Margulies, Luise, 83
marriage, 17, 38–40
meals, 43–44
meat, 62–63
Memorias Antiguas Historiales del Peru (Montesinos), 75
men, 17
　see also army; ceremonies; farming; work
messengers, 81–82
metalworkers, 67
military. *See* army
minerals, 25, 64
mining, 25, 64, 65
Molina, Christoval de, 55, 66
money, 22
　see also accounting system; barter system; taxes
Montesinos, Fernando, 16, 75
Morris, Craig, 24, 25
Moseley, Michael E., 10, 18, 60
mummies, 46, 51
Murúa, Martin de, 14, 40, 51–52

Narrative of the Incas (Betanzos), 77, 78, 87
nature, as religious force, 46–48
navy, 75
nobility. *See* aristocracy

Ondegardo, Polo de, 27–28, 32, 66
ownership of land, 22

palaces, 40
Pizarro, Francisco, 14
　see also Spanish
poetry, 68–69
Poma, Huamán, 29, 30, 44, 81
potters, 66–67
power, 14–15, 21
prayers, 54
priests, 51–54
Principe, Rodrigo Hernández, 56

Index 107

rebellion, 32–33, 78
reciprocity, 22
recordkeeping, 65–66
recreation, 44
relics, 46
religion, 46–59, 90, 92
religious leaders, 51–54
resettlement, 32
rituals. *See* ceremonies
roads, 13, 80–83
   see also construction; transportation
Rostworowski de Diez Canseco, María, 19, 22, 72
Rowe, John Howland, 37, 56
Royal Commentaries of the Incas and General History of Peru (Garcilaso), 62, 67
ruler. *See* emperor
runners, 81–82
   see also communication; transportation

sacred objects, 49
   see also religion
sacrifice, 54–56
Sancho, Pedro, 65, 90
sanitation, 41–42
schooling, 26–27
servants, 64–65
   see also common people

shrines. *See* temples
silversmiths, 67
size, 10
social customs, 34–45
   see also ceremonies; family; recreation; religion; work
social organization, 14–21
soldiers, 27
Spanish, 11, 92–94
spinning, 42
spirits, 48–49
sports, 44, 45
spying, 75
stonemasons, 84, 85–87
Stone-Miller, Rebecca, 32, 94
stones as sacred objects, 49
stonework, 84, 85–87
storehouses, 22, 23–25, 73–74, 90

taxes, 26–27, 28, 64–66
temples, 49–51, 83–84, 90
terraces, 90–91
   see also farming
textiles, 45
Thompson, Donald E., 24, 25
trade, 22, 25–26
transportation, 14, 25–26, 66, 72–74
   see also communication; roads
treasury, 22
trials, 30

Virgins of the Sun, 52–54, 57

warehouses, 22, 23–25, 73–74, 90
warfare. *See* army
weapons, 76–78
weather, 60
weaving, 42, 44, 45
Wise, Karen, 89
women, 17, 27–28, 42, 51–54, 62

   see also ceremonies
wool, 42
work, 60–69
   see also specific types of work
Wright, Kenneth R., 80, 85

Zegarra, Alfredo Valencia, 80, 85
Zuidema, R. Tom, 20

Picture Credits

Cover Image: © The Art Archive/Chavez Ballon Collection Lima/Mireille Vautier
© Bettmann/CORBIS, 63
© Christie's Images/CORBIS, 19
© CORBIS, 76
Diseño Communications, 61
© Jim Erickson/CORBIS, 89
© Werner Forman/Art Resource, NY, 26, 31, 47, 66
© Michael Freeman/CORBIS, 41
© John Van Hasselt/CORBIS, 43, 93
© Historical Picture Archive/CORBIS, 55, 74
© Jeremy Horner/CORBIS, 27, 82
© Hulton Archive, 35
© Mark A. Johnson/CORBIS, 23
© Wolfgang Kaehler/CORBIS, 86
© Bildarchiv Preussischer Kulturbesitz/Art Resource, NY, 15, 83
© Mary Evans Picture Library, 39
© Reuters/CORBIS, 53, 73
Royalty-Free/CORBIS, 58
© Francesco Venturi/CORBIS, 50
© Pablo Corral Vega/CORBIS, 11

About the Author

James A. Corrick has been a professional writer and editor for twenty years and is the author of twenty-five books, as well as two hundred articles and short stories. Other books he has written for Lucent are *The Early Middle Ages, The Late Middle Ages, The Renaissance, The Industrial Revolution, The Civil War: Life Among the Soldiers and Cavalry, The Louisiana Purchase, Life of a Medieval Knight, The Incas,* and *The Civil War.* Along with a PhD in English, Corrick's academic background includes a graduate degree in the biological sciences. He has taught English, edited magazines for the National Space Society, and edited and indexed books on history, economics, and literature for academic presses. He and his wife live in Tucson, Arizona.

The New School @ South Shore
8825 Rainier Ave. South
Seattle, WA 98118